'Stand and Deliver!'

– Stories of Irish Highwaymen

'Stand and Deliver!'

– Stories of Irish Highwaymen

Jim McCallen

Mercier Press Ltd
PO Box 5, 5 French Church Street, Cork *and*
24 Lower Abbey Street, Dublin 1

© The estate of Jim McCallen, 1993

ISBN 1 85635 036 3

A CIP catalogue record for this book
is available from the British Library.

Acknowledgements

I would like to express my thanks to the various organisations and people who assisted me in researching material for this book. Information on many of the outlaws was extremely difficult to find, and numerous individuals were particularly generous with their help and encouragement. Of particular help were:

> Belfast Central Library, Newtownards Library, Irish Department Ballynahinch Library, Post Office Archives London, Linenhall Library, Irish World Heritage Centre Donaghmore.

Printed in Ireland by Colour Books Ltd.

BEV

Contents

It is said that places have a soul. Even when they become deserted and no longer used by man, the places retain their souls. The soul is kept alive through the memory and oral tradition of the community. Songs, ballads and poems, together with the myths and legends are passed from generation to generation, until they become blurred with the truth and merge into the culture of the area. Tories, rapparees and highwaymen are part of Ulster's culture.

Introduction

IN IRELAND DURING the 1700s there were hundreds of highwaymen. Why, in a time when the penalty was hanging and having your head spiked, were so many men prepared to run that risk?

The existence of such a great number of highwaymen may be explained by the so-called Plantation of Ireland in 1608, when the land was being given to English and Scottish settlers. These landlords in turn leased the land to the Irish tenant farmers. Rents were so high that tenants could only afford to lease small unprofitable farms. Often these tenants never saw money. To pay the rent they would work on the landlord's estate and he had the right to demand labour when he needed or wanted it.

In the bitter angry years after the Battle of the Boyne, landlords frequently increased or even doubled the rents, thus leading to evictions. When the bailiffs turned up at the cottage, there were often scuffles and a bailiff or policeman might be injured. In such cases, a price could be put on the head of the man who had inflicted the injury. He would be forced to go on the run.

When men had to leave home for reasons such as these they often became highwaymen or rapparees. Local people said they 'went on their keeping'. Some, for a brief period, like flickering candles, achieved notoriety. The most 'successful' were the gentlemen highwaymen like Ness O'Haughan who robbed rich landowners, gave money to the poor tenants to help them pay their rent, and then robbed the rent agents.

The government put up a reward of £5 for information regarding highwaymen. That would have been four months wages for men for whom money was very short. It was usually an old member of a gang or a close friend or relative who gave details to the officials. However, because of the reasons highwaymen had for turning to the roads and because of the financial support they sometimes gave the local people, they were often supplied with 'safe houses' in which to hide. It could, therefore, be a long time before officials caught up with them.

Hence, the eighteenth and early nineteenth centuries were times when travellers used the roads after dark at their peril.

Jim McCallen
Newtownards

~1~

Shane Crossagh

The Derry Outlaw

WHEN LAMPS ARE lit in winter and the nights are long and black, Shane Crossagh is still talked about around the firesides of Derry and Tyrone.

The wealth of folklore surrounding him indicates Shane's popularity during that period with town dwellers and country folk alike. He and his followers roamed the highways of the two counties around the beginning of the eighteenth century. He had many hide-outs in the thick forests that covered the Sperrins. One of his particular favourites was on Ben Braddagh.

From there, the outlaws would emerge, waylaying wealthy travellers, and relieving them of their valuables before disappearing into the mountains again. It was a life full of danger, excitement and occasional sadness. With the authorities constantly patrolling the hills ready to hunt down and shoot the tories, as they were known, the latter were willing to risk their lives to preserve their way of life.

Shane's real name was John O'Mullan. His father, a small farmer, had been evicted from his home at Faughan-vale by a rack-renting land agent. Consequently, the family retreated into the mountains and settled in a place called Lingwood, near Claudy. They were only one of many families in the area who had been driven from their homes to make way for the Planters. All of them had one thing in common – a justifiable anger and resentment at the treatment received at the hands of the English invaders. This wrath caused them to give support and shelter to the outlaws, protecting the wanted men from the authorities.

The name 'Crossagh', meaning 'pock-marked', probably originated with some ancestor bearing that blemish, but Shane himself had no such problem. His father, Donal, and his brothers also bore the distinguishing name which was probably to differentiate their family from numerous other O'Mullans in the west side of the Roe and Sperrin foothills. Shane, a tall, powerfully built man with dark hair and beard was known in some areas as 'John the left-handed striker', and became the local hero from Dervock to Strabane.

After their eviction the Crossagh family lived in a Spartan fashion. There was little money and the main – indeed sometimes the only – daily meal being stirabout, or porridge, Shane was not averse to hunting duck in the nearby bogs to supplement his meagre diet. His father had one cow which he grazed along the roadside to support his family. The feeding was poor but the family still lived in the hope of returning one day to their rightful home. Because of this, young Shane developed the habit of going back to the farm to keep the place tidy. New owners were not always interested in living on or near their new property and many farmsteads were allowed to fall into decay. In spite of strict warnings from the authorities to stay away from the place, the Crossaghs had no intention of seeing their old home collapse through lack of interest.

It was this pride that almost cost Shane his life. One day he was spotted near the house and apprehended by two soldiers. They announced their intention of handing him over to the authorities and charging him with trespassing. Shane knew it was pointless to struggle. He did the next best thing.

'It's bad enough that I can't keep an appointment with a friend,' he complained. 'But I'd like to take the poteen with me if you have no objection.'

'Let us have it and we'll not put you in irons,' offered the soldiers.

Shane pretended to retrieve the poteen from its hiding place in some bushes. Instead, he pulled out a pike he had earlier concealed and turned to challenge the two men. Taken by surprise, the men decided that the best course of action was to drop their pistols and leave the scene, and Shane, as rapidly as possible.

It was an action which changed his whole life.

When he told his father what had happened, there was an immediate rush to contact some friends who might provide a hiding place. It was no idle panic. In those days, no one threatened the military and got away with it. It was certain that the soldiers would report Shane's attack, and an inevitable order would be made for his arrest. From that moment, Shane faced the possibility of death by hanging.

A meeting was held in the Crossagh home attended by Dominic the schoolmaster, Roddy the Irish soldier, Paddy Fada and a couple of farmers. Lookouts had been posted to alert them to any sign of approaching soldiers. All those present knew that time was short. Of the few options open to Shane, none seemed very attractive. The schoolmaster advised him to go to the local magistrate at once.

Shane was against it. As far as he was concerned, the

magistrate would side with the soldiers.

It was pointed out that, according to the law, Shane had been trespassing.

'But he is still young enough to pretend ignorance,' argued the schoolmaster. 'If he returns the two pistols he took from the soldiers and admits his mistake, they might take a lenient view. Then he can ask for a pardon.'

'I will ask for no pardon,' declared Shane. 'I did nothing wrong. I was looking after the family property that they took from us. It was they who were trespassing. It is our land.'

'We know you did nothing wrong, Shane,' agreed Dominic, 'but we have to live under English laws and English lawmakers. Now is not the time to fight them. We are not strong enough. And besides, they have all the weapons. You must ask for mercy.'

'It's your only chance,' agreed Shane's father. 'Even though I hate to admit it, Dominic is right. He has your interests at heart.'

'I won't do it,' argued Shane. Despite his youth, he had heard many tales about the treatment handed out to those who broke the law. His pride was also at stake and it was not easy for a young man to plead mercy from people who had taken his land away from him. The arguments he had listened to had strengthened his resolve to stand firm.

'It's either ask for mercy, or take to the hills,' added Paddy. 'The least that can happen to you is a few months in gaol. But you're young. You'd see the end of it.'

The arguments went far into the night. Shane was still prepared to hold his ground. Eventually, a neighbour brought word that the soldiers were searching for him. He realised his position was becoming more dangerous by the minute and his family would be at great risk if he stayed to fight. Dominic, who had seen many other young men like Shane being forced to go on their keeping outside the law, was anxious to help.

'If you like,' he offered, 'I'll go with you to the magistrate and speak on your behalf. It is my advice that we should submit to what we cannot mend.'

'Never,' said Shane. 'I will walk the ladder to the gallows before I submit to such tyranny. They will have to catch me before they put a rope round my neck. And before that happens, I'll make them remember Shane Crossagh.'

Paddy Fada and Roddy decided to join Shane. Together, they headed for the hills. Shane Crossagh had become an outlaw and rapparee, and so began the legend.

Before the Battle of the Boyne the word 'tory' was commonly used in connection with outlaws, but about this time the designation changed to rapparee, and even the term outlaw eventually fell into disuse.

The new description of rapparee crops up in the journals of John Steven and George Storey. The former was an adherent of King James; the latter was one of King William's chaplains. In Co. Armagh, it was in use as early as 1697, when a gentleman, wrote to his friend in Dublin that, '... yesterday about six of the clock in the afternoon, there came into this town a country fellow stripped to his shirt, with an account that Captain MacAnally and the rest of the rapparees that had so long infested this road had been caught while sleeping four miles from this place'.

The rapparees had posted a guard enabling the gang to put up a fight, but the unfortunate Captain MacAnally along with some of his men had been killed. Their heads were later displayed on spikes on the wall of the prison in the town. Such was the fate of any rapparee who was captured.

Shane's first den was cut out of turf – a round room with several bolt holes – at Craigbreac. Occasionally, he and his friends took shelter in the farm of Connolly Patchell.

His first known escapade as an outlaw illustrates some of the folklore surrounding him. One day, in the Maghera area, he called requesting food at the home of a widow. She offered him some milkless porridge, explaining that her only cow had been seized for rent that morning. The townlands of Beagh, Knocknakielt and Crew were at that time owned by a man called Mauleverer who was known to Shane. The next day he sought out the landlord, warning him to return the cow to the widow within a week or he would 'yoke him to a gig and drive him naked through the parish'. The landlord, not relishing the prospect, needless to say returned the cow, informing the authorities at the first opportunity.

Shane then proceeded to rob the local Protestant rector of £30, giving £10 to the widow to help with future expenses. This was the first of several similar incidents which enhanced Shane's reputation with the local people. No doubt the stories were greatly embellished in the telling. The details of the first robbery are preserved in the ballad, 'The Widow's Tale', by James O'Kane of Gortinure, Maghera:

> The widow saw a man outside her little cottage door;
> He seemed to her a stranger she never saw before;
> 'God save you kindly sir,' she said. 'God save you ma'am,' said he.
> 'Could you afford a bite and sup to Shane the Rapparee?'
>
> 'Come in, come in,' the widow cried, 'though scanty is my store;
> I've never sent a man away in hunger from my door;
> My humble fare with you I'll share and hope you'll be content;
> My only cow the landlord now has seized her for the rent.'

Shane listened to the widow's tale, such tales he'd heard
    before;
Said he, 'I'll share your humble fare, and God will send you
    more';
Said Shane, 'Perchance the greedy brute some night will meet
    with me;
If he can run, then I can shoot,' said Shane the Rapparee.

Shane stole out through the widow's door, just at the dawn of
    day;
He left a guinea on the floor, before he went away.
He scorned to keep the public road, as minions of the Crown
In ambush lay both night and day to hunt Shane Crossagh
    down.

I've read an ancient manuscript of legendary lore,
And found the landlord, he was robbed one night at Tober-
    more;
I cannot tell by whom or how, yet shanachies agree;
He handed o'er his golden store to Shane the Rapparee.

And if you meet a shanachie he'll tell you when and how
The poor old widow Donaghy possessed another cow.

It is said that Mauleverer's ghost still haunts Maghera. His
home was on the Grillagh road out of Maghera and his
ghost can often be seen at night near the spot where he once
lived. He was Sheriff of the county in 1740. His son, Belling-
ham Mauleverer was rector of Ballinascreen, and later of
Maghera and Bovevagh.

In Shane's time, a landlord's word could hang a man.
Shortly after helping the widow, Shane was arrested and
brought before the landlord and the rector. He was convicted and ordered to be taken to Derry gaol. On Palm Sunday
morning, Shane, fettered and manacled, began his long walk
along the old road that cut across Carntogher mountain. By
midday his military escort was tired and hungry enough to
halt by the roadside to have something to eat. We shall
never know whether Shane suggested the idea or one of the

soldiers, but the platoon of men began trying to outjump each other in a friendly competition. Shane managed to persuade them to allow him to participate, and they removed his shackles. They then formed a loose cordon round him to prevent any possible escape.

They had forgotten that Shane was not wearing the heavy boots and uniform of a soldier and, with a sudden dash, he broke through the cordon and headed across country. The soldiers gave chase, some of them even trying to shoot and reload as they ran, but he was too fast. The men had lost too much time sorting themselves out after his initial dash for freedom. They chased him for almost ten miles but he gave them the slip for a time by swimming the River Bann and hiding among the bushes on the Antrim side where he concealed himself near the Largy Braes.

The military, however, was not to be shaken off so easily. They crossed the river farther upstream and continued the search. Shane by this time had had a chance to rest, and when they got too close, he went on the run again. Twice he narrowly missed being shot as the soldiers took more careful aim. He made his way through the Ness Glen and over Loughmore mountain to Slaghtmanus.

The troops, who were reasonably familiar with the countryside, could not help but feel pleased with developments. They began to forget their aching bodies. For months they had searched for the outlaw, on occasion almost believing that he was able to make himself invisible. Now he was within sight. Running, jumping, scrambling over the land. At times he seemed to have wings on his feet. Each time they drew near, he got a new surge of energy and raced away from them again. But even Shane Crossagh could not keep going for ever. He was tiring.

They were closing in on him, convinced that he had pushed himself to the point of exhaustion. Added to that, his path was blocked by the fast-flowing Burntollet River. At that time the river jumped over rocks and crashed down into a deep gorge before tearing its way on through the valley. It looked like the end of the line for Shane.

He had little time to feel the fear that must have warned him not to jump. His legs were heavy and tired. His heart was pounding and he desperately wanted to rest. He was facing almost certain death. It was jump or be shot.

He jumped.

It was an incredible leap from the high bank to a narrow rocky ledge low down on the other side. Shane broke his leg in the process but managed to heave himself up the rocks and out of sight. When the soldiers arrived he was nowhere to be seen and they assumed that he had failed to cross the river and been drowned. In fact he made his way to a safe house where his injured leg was treated. He later headed into the Co. Antrim woods where he was met by some of his men. The woods were to become known as Shane's Woods, and the leap across the Burn Gushet, as Shane's Leap.

Shane continued to harass the rich planters, giving most of his own share of the plunder to the poor. In a strange way we could say that he initiated an early form of outdoor relief for the poor. He may even have believed in a redistribution of wealth. It is claimed by tradition that a family of landed gentry near Ballymoney asked for his help in securing for them what they had failed to obtain by legal process.

By now he had a dozen men in his gang, and he proceeded to levy a tax on every man of substance in the area. This was a common practice amongst rapparees, and ensured a regular income for the gang. If the farmer paid his tax –

in other words, protection money – he was guaranteed that no rapparee would rob him for the period covered by the 'tax'. Shane's fee was ten pence per quarter year.

For a time Shane and his men joined forces with another gang under the leadership of Paudreen McFaad, but Paudreen was too reckless for Shane, who avoided violence whenever possible. The only murder attached to his name was the killing of another highwayman. The victim had robbed a landholder under Shane's protection and refused to return the money. The two rapparees decided to settle the matter by open fight and Shane won.

There was no shortage of men anxious to join the rapparees. Life was not easy. There was always the risk of capture. Always the certainty after conviction of death by hanging. Public hangings were usually attended by great crowds. These gatherings served two purposes. The authorities used them to impress on those present the futility of breaking the law. The people used them as a public demonstration of support for the rapparees by cheering every word they uttered before they were executed.

Shane had a price on his head, but he was regarded as a champion of the people and every door was open to him. The patrols were increased and the military imposed severe punishment on anyone suspected of hiding him, or supplying him with food. He was by now a married man with two sons, Paudreen and Rory, who rode with him. They rode far and wide, raiding and ambushing, always managing to avoid capture by an enthusiastic, if frustrated, military.

One night the gang split up to find shelter in various safe houses from the torrential rain. Shane, his two sons and Paudreen McFaad made their way to Charlie Fowler's Inn, about a mile outside the town of Dungiven. They were well known to the landlord, who was also paying Shane protection money. It was not their first visit to the inn, and they used a small upstairs room, directly above the bar. From here it was easy to listen to the conversations of travellers without being seen. It was a method Shane had often used before to identify wealthy travellers on their way back from the markets, later relieving them of their money.

That night, General Napier and a troop of cavalry decided to rest at the inn before proceeding to Derry the next day. The general enjoyed his dinner and before long joined in conversation with some of the other guests. The drink was plentiful and as tongues loosened, the topic of conversation focused on how the country was being terrorised by rapparees. The general became very angry at what he saw as '... the negligence of the magistrates and authorities in allowing the Crossagh scoundrel to maraud the land'.

He was convinced that the outlaws had frightened the magistrates into leaving them alone. A stranger to modesty, he boasted that, given the chance, he would have Crossagh's head on a pike within the week.

Shane overheard the boasting of the general and, along with his three companions, slipped out of the inn during the night to prepare an ambush. He selected a long narrow bridge about half a mile from Feeny and his men took up positions. Shortly after dawn, as the troop of cavalry, headed by the general, trotted on to the bridge Shane shot Napier's horse from under him. In the confusion that followed, the troops were unable to manoeuvre on the narrow bridge, and their retreat was prevented by Shane's sons. The soldiers were ordered to dismount and stack their muskets while Napier was directed to surrender his sword or die. This done, the horses were led off the bridge while the troops were told to strip down to their underwear. They were then tied in pairs and ordered to march the rest of the way to their headquarters in Derry.

Shane saved an extra insult for the general. He forced him to dress in the clothes of a woman and walk at the head of his company, escorted, part of the way by Shane and his men. The scene of the ambush became known as the 'General's Bridge'. In later raids, Shane used the army uniforms to cause confusion within the ranks of the military. An old ballad commemorates the episode:

> One flash of his musket – the General wheeled round,
> And the steed and his rider both rolled on the ground;
> His guardsmen they gaped with a panic-struck stare,
> When the voice of Shane Crossagh roared loud in the air
> 'Surrender, ye knaves, to true knights of the pad,
> The strong hand for ever – and Paudreen McFaad.'
>
> 'Now oaths wildly sounded, and pistols went flashing,
> And horses high bounding, and broad swords all clashing;
> The demon of plunder in glory did revel,
> For Shane and stout Paudreen laid on like the devil,
> Till at length fairly routed, the whole scarlet squad
> Were tied neck and heels by bold Paudreen McFaad.

The enormous reputation of Shane led also to many imitators. Hold-ups and raids were carried out in his name and there were many false claims of his death when these impostors were shot. On one occasion he stayed the night in the home of a man who was planning to leave at three o'clock in the morning for the fair at Claudy. The man left as planned, leaving Shane alone in the house, but had only gone a few miles when he was stopped by a highwayman.

'Your money or your life,' said the outlaw. 'This is Shane Crossagh who demands it.'

The traveller had no choice but to give his money away.

When he reached the fair he was stopped by Shane himself who returned the money to him.

'You were good enough to give me lodgings,' said Shane. 'And I followed you to make sure you got here safely. The man who stole from you will bother you no more.'

Some of the attacks carried out in Shane's name have been attributed to individual members of his band, trying to make a reputation for themselves. Still others have been blamed on another rapparee called Rory Roe O'Haran who operated in the same area. Shane too, is often associated with the exploits of other highwaymen such as Roddy Dempsey of Baranilt.

Like many men in his profession, Shane Crossagh lived by a distinct code of honour. He would not steal from the poor. He robbed only the wealthy settlers and was against violence. He always repaid a debt. A family called McCurdy gave him shelter when he was being chased by blood-hounds, an action that saved his life. During a subsequent spate of cattle stealing, the McCurdy family were not molested. When one of the McCurdy children fell into the River Roe, he was saved by 'a big man with a beard who said his name was Shane'.

Nevertheless, time was slowly running out for Shane Crossagh. The army, now in greatly increased in numbers, was combing the hills for him. He could only move with great stealth and the owners of 'safe houses' were already being put in gaol for supporting him. Some members of his band of followers had been caught and executed. Shane had disguised himself and attended their execution. The future seemed bleak, and the leg he had broken at 'Shane's Leap' was causing him a lot of pain. Countless nights of hiding in rain-soaked bushes had led to the onset of rheumatism. He could no longer move as quickly or as quietly as in the old days.

It was a local weaver from Dungiven who finally sprung the trap that caught the outlaw. Acting under instructions of a magistrate, the weaver agreed to allow the military to hide on his land when Shane next called to collect his levy of ten pence. When the rapparee called, the weaver told him to get it out of a drawer near the door. Unsuspecting, Shane took the money and left the cottage. Before he had travelled twenty yards, the military rushed out of hiding and surrounded him. When he demanded to know what charge they would put against an innocent traveller, the weaver announced that he was willing to swear that Shane had stolen ten pence from his house.

Some reports claim that the weaver had betrayed Shane because they had once been rivals in a love affair in which Shane won his wife. Whatever the truth, the outcome was inevitable. Shane was shackled and taken to Derry gaol. A few days later his sons were apprehended when they came to look for him. They joined him in gaol and all three were later convicted of theft, and sentenced to death by execution.

Shane, now in his fifties and considered old for a man in his profession, had made many friends during his lifetime. The Irish people who had been dispossessed of their lands had no chance of saving their hero's life, because they had no power or influence. But one man, the son of a planter, did have some political influence. Shane had, some years earlier, saved the life of Henry Carey, originally from north Devon, who lived in Dungiven Castle and had the right to grant a reprieve to one criminal each year. He attempted to exercise this right on Shane's behalf. Shane was offered his life.

'Will my sons be spared too?' he asked.

When he was told that they must die, he declined the offer of a pardon.

'I have only a few years left to live in any case,' he said. 'I cannot be long after them. So, with God's blessing, I'll die with them.'

According to the testimony of the Reverend John Low, Presbyterian minister of Banagher, who witnessed the execution, Shane died with a son on each side of him, holding each by the hand. There was a large crowd at the execution and this act made him a hero in their eyes. The scaffold of the old Derry gaol in the Diamond at the top of the hill, saw the end of one of the most remarkable and popular rapparees in the history of the county.

One of the customs of the time was to allow the condemned man to speak to the people from the scaffold. With his hands clasping those of his sons, his legs in shackles and the noose about his neck, the tall gaunt, bearded man looked round at the faces before him and straightened his shoulders. He then proceeded to thank them for the support they had given him over the years. He asked that they remember him with kindly thoughts and in their prayers. When the cheering had stopped, he said that if anyone was present from Dungiven, they should look for a foalskin of guineas between 'a gentle bush in Termeil and a standin' stone in Derrychrier'. With a final look at his two sons, he nodded to the hangman. Minutes later the Derry Outlaw was dead.

Relatives from Tamnagh, Dreen and Ballydonegan claimed the bodies. The year of his execution was 1722. In a letter written by William Nicholson, Protestant Bishop of Derry from 1718–26 it is stated: 'The present insolence of our Popish clergy is unspeakable. Our laws makes it death for them to officiate, yet I am abundantly assured that very lately in my own diocese, four or five masses were openly said over the corpse of an executed robber, whose funeral rites were celebrated with as pompous and as numerous attendances as if the man had died knight of the shire....'

Shane Crossagh and his sons were buried in Banagher old church graveyard.

~2~

Cushy Glen

From Murder Hole Road

HONOUR WAS SOMETHING foreign to Cushy Glen. He cared neither for courtesy nor chivalry. Many of those who met him never lived to tell the tale, others regretted their expensive encounter with the man from Murder Hole Road.

No doubt he had heard of highwaymen who became folk heroes in their day, but judging from his particular lifestyle, it seems he regarded his professional peers as weak and foolish.

If he had lived perhaps fifty years earlier, he might well have had different standards, or joined one of the many gangs that roamed the countryside. But Cushy made a name for himself towards the end of the eighteenth century when the days of the highwaymen were numbered.

His trademark was violence and murder.

There were still petty thieves and robbers about in Cushy's day, but the state was now better organised and the military more efficient. The authorities had learned by experience the skills of the outlaws and were able more accurately to predict the methods of those remaining beyond the law. Consequently, the chances of capture were much greater. The local people too, were slowly adopting, albeit reluctantly, the new ways and there was less support for the outlaws. As communications had improved, the highwayman was forced to change his tactics or live a very short life.

Furthermore, there were no outstanding law-breakers with the charisma of Redmond O'Hanlon, the Brennans, or James Freney. If there had been a few of the more successful names around, then the old-style highwayman would have lasted a little longer. But times were changing. The more daring in the community were now seeking reform through secret societies such as the Whiteboys, the Hearts of Oak, and the United Irishmen.

Cushy was caught between the old and the new and could not fit comfortably into either style.

Where his predecessors had used skill and cunning, he used simple confrontation and death. Where the old-style highwayman generally had the respect, if not the full support of the people, Cushy remained a shadowy figure and was shunned by the community.

One of the last, and perhaps the most chivalrous old-style knights of the road was James Freney from Kilkenny, who refused to rob any woman, and who always ensured that his wealthy victims were left with enough money to defray immediate expenses until reaching the end of their journey.

On one occasion, he was in the process of emptying a man's pockets when a thimble was discovered amongst the gold and silver. On learning that the man was a mere tailor he returned everything to him and sent him on his way. Part of an old ballad illustrates the reputation of Freney:

One morning as I being free from care
I rode abroad to take the air;
'Twas my fortune for to spy
A jolly Quaker riding by.
And it's oh, bold Captain Freney!
Oh, bold Freney oh!

Says the Quaker, 'I did not think
That you would play me such a roguish trick;
As my breeches I must resign
I think you are no friend of mine'.
And it's oh bold Captain Freney!
Oh, bold Freney oh!

As we rode a little on the way,
We met a tailor dressed most gay
I boldly bid him for to stand,
Thinking he was some gentleman.
And it's oh bold Captain Freney oh!
It's bold Freney oh.

Upon his pockets I laid hold –
The first thing I got was a purse of gold;
The next thing I found which did me surprise,
Was a needle, thimble and chalk likewise.
And it's oh, bold Captain Freney oh!
It's bold Freney oh.

'Your little trifle I disdain,'
With that returned his gold again;
'I'll rob no tailor if I can –
I'd rather ten times rob a man'.
And it's oh, bold Captain Freney oh!
It's bold Freney oh.

On another occasion he robbed a Mr Anderson, who collected hearth money in the neighbourhood. When he learned the man's profession, he immediately returned the money in order to prevent the man losing his job.

Freney was pardoned in 1750, and obtained a job as a tide-waiter at the port of New Ross. He is buried in Innistogue churchyard.

Cushy Glen would not have been considered for a pardon. It is most unlikely he would have even considered asking for such a thing. To obtain a pardon, a highwayman needed friends with influence. Cushy had neither friends nor influence. Yet he was never apprehended or brought to trial for his offences.

Cushy served for a time in the army in Derry. His wife, Kitty, was employed as a cook in the army kitchens. From what little is known about him, he was a short burly man with 'a brown complexion, very much marked with smallpox and repulsive looking'.

After a period in the army he was dismissed and, together with his wife, set out to make a life for himself as a small farmer. With little skill and hardly any money, he soon realised that there were easier and faster ways to make a living.

Any knowledge he had gleaned from his time in the army revolved round horses and weapons. He could not afford a horse, but he did have a gun – the essential tool for the trade of a highwayman.

Following a well known practice, he began his career in crime by stealing from local landlords. At first it was the occasional duck, or hen, sometimes vegetables and meal. Then he progressed to breaking into their homes. A few close shaves with the military and narrowly missing being shot dead, convinced him that his particular talents lay in other directions.

At the end of the eighteenth century and early years of the nineteenth century, hand spinning and hand loom weaving were popular sidelines amongst the agricultural community of Ulster. Almost every farmer who grew flax or grazed sheep wove his own linen or woollen cloth which found a ready market in the towns.

The men often found themselves with a substantial amount of money in their possession which, in turn, was a great temptation to the highway robbers and thieves who also frequented the market places. Once a victim had been identified, the thieves would hide somewhere along the journey home and relieve the traveller of anything valuable he might be carrying on his person. Despite more efficient military patrols, communication was still relatively primitive and slow and it was impossible to provide escorts for every traveller. Consequently, the thieves had plenty of time to make a getaway. By the time the ambush had been reported to the military, the outlaw's trail was very cold.

A group of men operating under the leadership of a man called Joe Scott is a good example of the new style of outlaw. His gang was a rough group of individuals who never really worked as a closely knit team. When it came to collective planning and objectives, it was a case of every man for himself. Joe tried to make them into a gang. He had dreams of emulating Redmond O'Hanlon or Shane Crossagh, but lacked their commanding presence. The men had no respect for him. The only thing that held them together as a group for a time was their collective greed and a need for easy money. The gang attacked travellers going to and from market, but he did not specialise in hold-ups. Isolated farmhouses and cottages were all likely to receive his attention. Even the odd shebeen had been subjected to one of his not-too-friendly visits.

The local community as well as the military was sick and tired of his attacks. At least one man was prepared to stand up to the gang. On a cold, wet night, Joe and his gang attacked a house with the intention of taking whatever food and money might be available. Joe made the mistake of believing the sight of his gang would frighten the inhabitants into submission, and he dismounted in the yard. At the top of his voice he demanded immediate entry into the house – and got a bullet in the head.

James Henry had never considered himself a brave man but his reaction made him an overnight hero. He shot Joe dead and fired another shot in the direction of the gang. Joe's companions, after a brief moment of indecision, demonstrated their courage by galloping off into the night, thankful to have escaped with their lives.

Joe Scott was no longer of this world, but Mr Henry waited until daylight before venturing out to check on the condition of the outlaw. There was always the chance, according to Mr Henry, that the gang might come back, or wait for him to come out of the house before launching another attack.

He need not have worried.

The gang were probably still running and Joe had gone where all baddies go!

Joe's body was put on public display, and Mr Henry was granted a special lease on his house in recognition of his bravery in ridding the country of one who, with his followers, had been the scourge of the community for years.

Needless to say, the authorities were delighted and for a time it was thought that the countryside had seen the last of the highwaymen. Men who had taken to travelling in groups for protection and self-preservation began to risk riding on their own again.

Eventually reports began to arrive at army headquarters about the disappearance of respectable businessmen. While there was no evidence that Scott's gang was responsible for the disappearance of these men, it was widely assumed that they had returned to the area and resumed their activities. Robberies continued and more people who travelled by the old coach road between Coleraine and Limavady simply vanished.

At this time, the only road connecting the two towns was a narrow switch-back, lane-like road of mud and stones. In dry weather, it was usable but only with care and difficulty. After a shower of rain or snow, the surface became slippery and even dangerous for riders.

The countryside was bleak and desolate; the lone traveller was surrounded by an eerie stillness as he went on his journey. Not a route for the faint-hearted, even in daylight, this hump-backed road wound its way between vast areas of bogland, and a cold wind that blew from the Keady mountains chilled limbs of horse and man alike. Even the occasional haunting sound of the curlew was swallowed up in the wind, and the cry of the gulls, wheeling and drifting above the land, was disturbing and frightening.

The place was one of utter desolation.

There were many theories put forward for the disappearance of the travellers. Ghosts and witches were the most popular. Scott's old gang was suspected by the military, but in fact they were as terrified as everybody else. It was even suggested that the missing men had been kidnapped and press-ganged.

During the Napoleonic wars, ships at anchor off Greencastle were believed to send press gangs ashore to the Magilligan district, where smugglers also abounded. Following the rebellion in 1798, the Coleraine district experienced very disturbed conditions and it was felt by some that the disappearances were the settling of old scores. No one at the time thought of investigating the inhabitants of a lonely cottage near the Sconce Hill. No one asked themselves how the man and woman who lived there made enough money to survive in what was little more than a mud hut.

Cushy Glen and his wife, Kitty, were surviving quite well. This highwayman was no Robin Hood. He was careful enough to pretend that he was living, like many others, in dire poverty. In fact, Cushy and his wife were making a business out of murder.

From the door of his cottage, Cushy was able to see an approaching traveller while he was still some distance away. The outlaw then took up his usual position near a hollow by the roadside, about six miles from Coleraine. After killing the unfortunate traveller, he would empty the victim's pockets and bury the body in the hollow. It was later learned that he had the enthusiastic help and support of Kitty in the proceedings. It was a macabre partnership and, for a period, quite profitable. The total amount of gold and silver, together with bolts of cloth and other valuables that Cushy stole, has never been accurately assessed. It is, however, reasonable to assume that the couple could well have afforded to move to more comfortable surroundings.

Cushy was a man of few ambitions. As far as he was concerned, business was good and there was no need to move or risk embarrassing questions. They had no children and their expenses were unlikely to rise. Their future seemed secure. They were not harassed by the authorities and it seemed as if their operation was totally foolproof.

Whether or not either of them ever gave serious thought to the fact that times were changing, or that the 'good' life would end, is impossible to judge. We do know that by 1804, Cushy's days were numbered.

A young man by the name of Harry Hopkins travelled to Coleraine one day to sell his cloth in the market. As he laid the webs over his horse's back, in packsaddle fashion, he had no idea that he was about to create his own little piece of history.

He had no difficulty in selling the material in the market, and spent the rest of the day renewing friendships and catching up with the gossip. He also purchased some goods for his home, unwittingly demonstrating the fact that he was carrying a large amount of money. It was during the late afternoon that he became aware that one man seemed to be following him. At first he dismissed thoughts of frequent glimpses of the stranger as mere coincidence, but there was a certain unease at the back of his mind that the stranger had some ulterior motive for his actions.

Harry was well aware of the dangers he faced on the journey home, but he was fairly satisfied that highwaymen were less of a threat than in his father's time. Despite his optimism, he mentioned the stranger to the landlord at the inn where his horse was stabled.

The landlord was concerned enough to advise Harry to spend the night at the inn and wait for daylight before returning home. The young man, however, was determined to reach home that night and, rather than delay any longer, he borrowed a pistol from the landlord and headed out of the town.

Shadows were deepening through the trees and the wild bogland stretched away from the road and lay on top of itself in fold upon fold. Even the birds were silenced now as the night closed in. Harry was fearful and began to wish that he had taken the landlord's advice. Every now and again he stopped and listened to the silence all about him. There were no following hoof-beats. His own mount seemed to feel his unease and became nervous and difficult to control. It was as though the animal sensed danger in the darkness of the night.

Harry talked to the horse, trying to calm it down as they negotiated the mile-long gradient over the shoulder of the Sconce Hill. It was normally a well-behaved animal, but it was strangely nervous.

Suddenly, out of the night, a figure materialised beside the road and grabbed the bridle. Harry was startled and struggled to regain control of the frightened horse.

'Stand and deliver!' said the figure.

The horse was still trembling. Harry could see the pistol levelled at him and reached into an inside pocket as though to obey the outlaw. Instead of withdrawing his purse, however, he gripped his own pistol and fired through his coat at almost point-blank range. The figure staggered and collapsed, and the horse, terrified by the explosion, broke into a wild gallop.

Good sense made Harry allow the horse its head and he clung on for dear life. For all he knew, there were associates of the outlaw close at hand. It was a dangerous ride. The road was nothing more than a rough track, and a fall could have killed both horse and rider. Harry did not care. He only wanted to put as much distance as possible between himself and the outlaw. The wind pulled at his clothes and his hat flew into the night, but still he galloped down the hill. He heard a woman's voice shouting, 'Did you get him, Cushy?'

Harry did not stop to answer.

Early next day, Harry returned to the scene with a number of men from Limavady. He was anxious to learn the identity of his assailant and he had already told them about the woman's voice. There was no police in those days, but the local magistrate had the power to order men to assist him. It was these 'deputies' who accompanied Harry.

They found that the body – later identified as that of Cushy Glen – had been dragged to the side of the road and abandoned. By its side they found a loaded pistol and a short sword cutlass. The men immediately hurried to surround the cottage, hoping to capture Cushy's wife. But the bird had flown.

No trace of Kitty Glen has ever been found.

The full extent of Cushy's crimes is impossible to estimate as he was blamed for the disappearance or death of more than a score of men. However, in a search of the area near his home, the bodies of twelve people in various stages of decomposition were discovered. Most of them were in a common grave in a hollow close to the road. Only a few of the unfortunate victims could be identified. This is how the road came to be known locally as the Murder Hole Road.

It was some time before travellers again felt safe enough to travel on the road between Coleraine and Limavady. A few clung to the belief that Kitty Glen would seek some sort of revenge on the community for the death of her husband. With time, however, Cushy's hut collapsed and only the shell remained to remind people of 'the old days'.

Eventually, even Kitty was forgotten. It would be interesting to know if she took all the stolen money with her. Did she remain in Ulster? Or did other lands attract her?

Today, even on a bright summer day, there are those travellers who claim to sense a strange haunting atmosphere as they approach the Sconce Hill. They say it is a place where the wind is never warm and the ghost of Cushy Glen never far away.

~3~

Black Francis

TOWARDS THE END of the eighteenth century, the outlaw Proinnsias Dubh – one of Ulster's most famous rapparees – and his gang roamed all over Fermanagh, Tyrone and Donegal. At this time, the small farmers, particularly those in the more mountainous areas, lived in extreme poverty with little food and hardly any money. They eked out a miserable existence in wretched hovels made of mud and stone, without windows or doors. Sometimes the opening contained a wattle door covered with a straw mat on the inside as a meagre shield against the wind and rain.

Almost all of these people had been dispossessed by the planters. Now most of the income from their labours went to fill the pockets of the landlords. To supplement their income, many farmers hired themselves out to the landlords and worked on land they themselves had previously owned.

As the young men grew into manhood, their resentment made them look for ways of improving the quality of their lives. The exploits of the rapparees gave hope to the poor, and presented the young with heroes to emulate.

However, many young men had short careers. They lacked experience, horses and weapons. They had no idea how to deal with a platoon of soldiers or a troop of cavalry sent out to bring them back dead or alive. Despite their intimate knowledge of the country, they were often easily and quickly captured and ended up on the gallows.

Some did survive for a time, but few made their fortune, and even fewer lived long enough to make a name for themselves. One way to stay alive, at least for a reasonable period and in relative comfort, was to become a member of an established gang. And there was no lack of volunteers to join the rapparees hiding out in the mountains.

Black Francis was the leader of one of these roving bands of outlaws who, for a time, lived well and were a law unto themselves, always on the run from the authorities, constantly moving from hide-out to hide-out, often using 'safe houses' when the military got too close. It was a life-style that suited a special kind of person. To lead a band of individuals who feared not even death, required a uniquely strong and courageous character. Such a man was Black Francis. He lived by the creed of the old Cretan warriors:

> My word, my spear, my shaggy shield,
> They make me lord of all below,
> For he who dreads the lance to wield,
> Before my shaggy shield shall bow,
> His lands, his vineyards, must resign,
> And all that cowards have is mine.

Black Francis was born about five miles from Pettigo, in the townland of Cloghure, in the parish of Termonamangan. His parents had been small farmers in the early days. He was a broad, stockily built man with dark hair and bushy beard. Proinnsias got his first lesson in stealing from a man he met at Dungeon Quarries, outside Castlederg. The man was on his way to Dundalk and helped young Proinnsias carry a bag of oaten meal from Strabane to his home, a distance of about sixteen miles. The two became quite friendly and the man stayed with the family a few days before continuing his journey. During his stay he taught Proinnsias how to get his oaten meal for nothing. It was the first step for Proinnsias into what became a relatively profitable career in crime.

No doubt the family derived benefit from his newly acquired skill, but it was not long before the youth grew tired of stealing oaten meal. He was a restless, angry, ambitious young man and was soon carrying out raids on the large landowners. He was adept at killing chickens and ducks, and his family ate well. By now his reputation was drawing some attention from the authorities who paid a number of visits to his home. They had their suspicions but always failed to obtain the necessary evidence to prove his guilt.

It was during one of their visits that Proinnsias got into an argument and hit one of the soldiers. For someone in his position this was a very serious offence and they tried to arrest him. Proinnsias knew what would happen to him once he was brought before the court, and took the only route possible. He ran from the house and headed for the hills. The troops, burdened down with their uniforms and weapons, were unable to catch him. When they reported the incident, Proinnsias was declared a wanted criminal.

He was forced to go on his keeping. Working alone, mostly under the cover of darkness, he made only occasional trips back home to see his family.

Gradually, he built a reputation for himself as a successful rapparee, and with it came men who were willing to follow him. So far his exploits had been directed against the landowners as they travelled to market, but he began to attack them in their homes where, he believed, most of their money would be kept. Anyone following him had to swear total allegiance and he became a powerful leader. The men generally associated with his gang were Tom Acheson, Tarlach Muireas, said to be a native of Tipperary, McQuade, McAlinn, Johnston, and 'Supple Dick' Corrigan. Proinnsias insisted that his followers obey two rules. First, only the rich were to be robbed. Second, no woman was to be offended or threatened.

Proinnsias used the mountainous district between Pettigo and Barnmore as his main base. Once in the hills he was almost impossible to find. The horses he used were of light build, active and sure-footed and capable of following the most difficult mountain track without stumbling.

An articulate and likable man, Proinnsias was friendly with the Achesons of Grouse Lodge in the heart of the mountains. The Achesons were on good terms with the monied people of the county and when a social evening was being held, frequently invited Proinnsias as a guest. On occasion, representatives of the authorities were also present, but the rapparee never declined an invitation. He became well known, under an assumed name, as an interesting visitor, but only the Achesons knew his real identity.

Proinnsias used these occasions to obtain information about the households and movements of other guests. He was not a drinking man and it was a relatively simple matter to collect details from those unable to hold their alcohol. In his profession it was important to know the dates when landlords would be away from their homes, and the exact number of servants. In this way he was able to carry out raids with the minimum of danger, and avoid the risk of his men being injured or captured.

One of the hallmarks of his work was the meticulous

planning of his various raids. He was so careful about planning that, on occasion, he was able to mount two raids at the same time. This level of expertise caused the army a great deal of trouble as their information was not always reliable, and much time was wasted when troops were sent to the wrong house.

One night, Proinnsias attended a function near the shores of Lough Erne, pretending to be a landlord from north-west Donegal. He claimed that his coach had broken down, and asked hospitality while it was being repaired. Some of his men were dressed as grooms and lackeys. What the other guests did not know was that the coach was concealed in nearby trees and had been stolen in an earlier raid. Other members of his gang were already hiding in the grounds of the estate. He then proceeded to entertain the guests with tales and songs, while his gang entered the house and stripped the upper storey of the house of its valuables. These were passed out to others who hid the goods in the coach. When the robbers entered the dining room, with pistols at the ready, Proinnsias was also 'robbed'.

Not all his attempts at robbery were successful. One December night he stopped a traveller on the Pettigo–Castlederg road and ordered him to hand over all his money. The stranger refused and threw himself at the rapparee. They were evenly matched and neither gained the upper hand in the fight. Finally, Proinnsias offered his hand.

'Stop all this nonsense. Let us shake hands and be friends. You are as good a man as I am. You are a brave man and I could have shot you. Good luck to you.'

It was an offer the traveller could not refuse.

He continued on his journey but, some distance along the road, was robbed by some of Proinnsias' men who had been waiting for his signal to join him. Later when the rapparee heard what they had done, he ordered them to ride after the unfortunate traveller and return his money.

Despite his strength as a leader and his apparently easygoing nature, Proinnsias, like every rapparee, was constantly under stress from the incessant attempts by the troops to capture him. In order to defend himself in case of an attack, he always slept with a loaded pistol under his pillow.

One night, tired and wet, he called at a safe house near the Barnsmore Gap and asked for a night's lodging. He advised the occupants not to let anyone else into the house and went to bed. Later that night, there was a loud thumping on the door. The woman of the house told the caller to go away but he forced his way into the room. Proinnsias, his nerves on edge, and half asleep, jumped out of bed and shot the stranger.

The family were panic-stricken, fearing that they would be blamed and punished for the killing.

'Tell them it was Proinnsias Dubh,' said the rapparee. 'And say I killed him for his horse.'

Even though Proinnsias planned his raids, there were times when the victims did not behave as expected.

One evening he received information that a traveller would be passing his way carrying a substantial amount of money, and Proinnsias set out to take it. He met a man called McCusker, returning from Donegal after collecting three years rent for a Dromore landlord. Proinnsias stopped him at a place called the Kerbies and demanded the money. McCusker refused and threw his bag over a precipice. The rapparee dismounted and climbed down the bank to retrieve the money. McCusker meanwhile grabbed the reins of the outlaw's horse and galloped off with both horses.

Because of recent heavy rain, Proinnsias had great difficulty in climbing the bank again, and by the time he reached the road, his men had arrived. The comments of Proinnsias on being made to look foolish are not recorded. His temper, however, would not have been helped by the fact that the bag of money he had gone to so much trouble to rescue, contained nothing more than stones. McCusker, it seemed, had sent the money by another route, while deliberately letting it be known which route he himself would be travelling.

An unusual feature of Proinnsias and his gang, was their habit of swooping down on the evening of a fair day into the street of a village, bringing with them an ample supply of poteen. Lookouts would be posted in case the military should arrive, and the whole community would adjourn to a field or barn and enjoy a dance. There were times when their dances were cut short by the arrival of patrols but, in general, the outlaws were rarely surprised.

Proinnsias kept a firm grip on the leadership of his gang and there is no indication that his position was ever seriously challenged. He was scrupulously fair in sharing out the takings of any raid and was quick to break up any disagreements within the gang. He operated a system whereby if any man had a grievance, it was heard in front of the whole gang where a verdict was reached based on a consensus. This meant that both sides of any argument felt they were given a fair hearing and no issues were left that might lead to demands for revenge, and a threat to the cohesion of the gang.

He maintained that the Ardnagapple Glen on the main road from Donegal to Derry yielded more money and profit to him than any other highway. He had acquired an intimate knowledge of the roads, even the times when travellers were most likely to use a particular road, and he was therefore able to pick the best spot for an ambush. In attempts to foil the highwaymen, travellers would often journey in well-armed groups, on their trips to market. Occasionally, Proinnsias would rob the whole group, but more often he would follow the travellers at a discreet distance and ambush them as they split up to go to their various homes.

The authorities too, were well aware of the gang's tactics and whenever possible would offer protection to the travellers. This was generally ineffectual and time-consuming. On such occasions, Proinnsias would simply let the procession pass by unmolested. On the rare occasion when Proinnsias or one of his men was careless enough to allow himself to be seen by the patrols, the army did give chase. But the heavily wooded slopes and steep paths were too familiar to the outlaws and escape was easy.

Very little of the loot stolen by Proinnsias and his men has ever been found. A substantial amount of the money went to the poor, sometimes as cash and sometimes as food.

Families opening their doors at night to an anxious knocking were often presented with a cow and a receipt for its purchase – with the compliments of Proinnsias Dubh. Others discovered in their barn meal and sections of slaughtered animals which had mysteriously arrived during the hours of darkness.

However, even allowing for the gang's share of the spoils, a great deal of silver ornaments, caskets of jewellery, cutlery, linens and other stolen items, simply disappeared. Perhaps descendants of the rapparees received them as gifts. An equally acceptable explanation is that much of the loot is still hidden among the rocks and crevices of some mountain pass. Tradition has it that one ruby, as big as an egg, was stolen from a wealthy landlord. Who knows what its value would be at today's prices?

Proinnsias was noted for his chivalry and, like the legendary knights of King Arthur, it was particularly obvious in his dealings with women. An example of this was when his gang robbed Lisgoole Abbey, and only the daughter of the house, Miss Pugh, and two servants, were present. They were tied and gagged while the gang went about the business of looting the house. On the way back to the hide-out, it was noticed that one of the men was missing and Proinnsias returned alone to the Abbey to investigate. He discovered not only that one of the servants had freed himself and gone for help, but in an upstairs room he found the missing member of his gang trying to undress the struggling Miss Pugh.

A fight broke out, during which Proinnsias knocked the man out by hitting him over the head with a pistol.

'I am Proinnsias Dubh,' he said to the young woman, 'and I apologise to you for the way you have been treated. You have my word he will be punished.'

By this time the military were entering the courtyard, but Proinnsias refused to leave the unconscious man. He heaved the body on to his shoulder and, some say with the help of Miss Pugh, hid in a wardrobe until the troops left.

During the search, the soldiers had found Proinnsias' horse and they took it with them when they departed.

When Proinnsias later headed out into the trees, it was approaching dawn and he had to carry the unconscious form of his companion some distance before he recovered. The two men then hid until daylight. By the time they reached camp it was close to midday. The rest of the gang were furious at the behaviour of their colleague and demanded that he be shot as a punishment.

Proinnsias, however, was against summary execution

even though he knew the man could no longer be trusted to be part of the gang.

'No,' he argued. 'We will discuss this after we have eaten. He will be allowed to put forward his defence and then we will decide. Enough of us are killed by the army without shooting each other.'

The men reluctantly accepted his decision and, by the time they had eaten, their tempers had cooled sufficiently to listen to both sides of the argument. In the end, it was decided to let him live but not to have him in the gang.

Proinnsias was pleased with the decision. He refused to give the offender his share of the robbery and ordered him to collect whatever things he owned in the camp, telling him that he was no longer a member of the gang.

'If you betray us, or even stay in this county,' he warned, 'you will be shot.'

The gang, of course, moved to a different hiding place a few days later and continued their business. Nothing more was ever heard of their former colleague.

As time passed, the strain began to take its toll on the gang. Mistakes were made, tempers became frayed and increased military activity forced them to be be even more vigilant. Proinnsias saw the changes in his men and tried to ease the strain by reducing the number of raids. He persuaded the men to lie low for a while, hoping that army searches would ease off. He was not entirely successful. Over the next few weeks three of his men were shot by the military in searches. Another was shot while taking part in a raid. Yet another man died when his horse fell on him.

As the number of patrols increased, greater rewards were offered for information leading to the arrest of the rapparees. Even safe houses were no longer a guarantee of safety. In a desperate attempt to protect his men, Proinnsias moved his band to Sligo and Galway. For a time everything went well for them and they raised the level of their activities again. But the countryside was not familiar to them. There were few safe houses. Added to this, the men were homesick and, while they were willing to obey Proinnsias and remain outside Ulster, he decided to head back to Fermanagh and familiar territory.

He was intelligent enough to realise that the odds were slowly mounting against them. On the way back to Ulster he must have turned over in his mind the possibility of retirement. He had had a good run, and he had enough money hidden away to make life easy for himself. Maybe he thought of the men who rode with him and who had stood beside him over the previous years.

He may have even felt responsible for them. They had followed his example and had obeyed his orders. They had risked their lives on his behalf and some of their number had even died under his command. Despite the dangers and the hardships, he had given them a sort of freedom. He could not let them down.

They returned to their old haunts.

The military increased its bribery, coercion and threats of eviction in its attempts to capture rapparees. These were not new steps. As early as 1655 courts had been set up to try, execute and punish not merely rapparees and those giving them support and shelter, but also those found not giving notice to the nearest garrison about the movement of any rapparees. Bribes and rewards had been used for a long time in the hunt for outlaws. In 'An abstract of all the monies received and paid for the public service in Ireland from July 1649, to November 1656', there occurs amongst the items:

Paid for killing wolves, £3,847, 5s, 0d.
Paid for apprehending rebels and Tories £2,149, 12s, 6d.

As the country was still generally covered with woods and bog, and settlers almost powerless to follow the outlaws with their minute knowledge of paths and tracks, the military authorities had little choice other than to try enlisting some of the native Irish. Some of this money was paid as 'head money' when the head of a rapparee was presented as proof of his death.

On 29 August 1670, the Sheriff of Co. Fermanagh, stated that he had 'paid on 4 July previous, at Coolaghtie in the said County, a Mr Millar and his friends who had killed and beheaded one Owen McGwire, a notorious tory, and had later received his head and immediately put it on public display'.

It was not long before the people of Fermanagh and Tyrone knew that Proinnsias and his men had returned. Travellers were stopped and relieved of their valuables. Some of the villages again got their supply of poteen on fair days, and complaints poured into the local garrison along with demands for the capture of Proinnsias Dubh.

In the end, it was a friend of Proinnsias who betrayed him. The man was called Hilliard and Proinnsias had paid him well over the years for information about the movement of the military. Hilliard was involved in running the local market and had also supplied the outlaw with details of who was carrying large sums of money, thus enabling planned ambushes to take place.

Hilliard and Supple Dick Corrigan had never liked each other. In fact, Corrigan had openly stated to Proinnsias that Hilliard was not to be trusted. He suspected that Hilliard was in the pay of the army and urged his leader not to rely on any further information the traitor might supply.

'Dick,' said Proinnsias, 'you and Hilliard have been my friends for years. I'm sorry there is this bitterness between the two of you.'

'I tell you he cannot be trusted,' argued Corrigan. 'He is working against us.'

'And I say that Jim Hilliard is one of us,' said Proinnsias. 'He has helped us many times in the past and it is my belief he will help us in the future. You are letting your imagination get the better of you. Where is your evidence? Give me proof and I will act on it.'

Proinnsias was wrong.

While Hilliard had accompanied Proinnsias and the gang on several occasions, he had recently been offered a pardon if he would help the military catch the outlaw. One night he informed the gang that the military was searching on the other side of the mountain and heading in the opposite direction. As a result of this message, when the men settled down for the night they posted no guards. It was a mistake that would cost Proinnsias his life.

Acting on information supplied by Hilliard, the military had moved into a position where they surrounded the camp. At midnight, the attack was launched. In the confusion that followed, both sides suffered casualties. The rapparees had been totally unprepared and only a few escaped into the darkness. One of them, Tom Acheson, who had been with Proinnsias from the early days, continued life as a rapparee at the head of his own gang for a few years. He was eventually captured and executed at Derry gaol.

Proinnsias and the others were shackled and marched into Enniskillen where he was separated from his men and thrown into a dungeon by himself. The shackles were not removed and he remained in solitary confinement for over a month while arrangements were made for his trial. Not that there could be any doubt about the outcome. His capture had been a great coup for the authorities and they wanted to make the most of it. They even put his coffin in the dungeon with him during the period of remand.

Proinnsias knew the sentence would be death. He had used arms against the forces of the Crown and he was a highwayman. He resigned himself to his fate and swore to die with dignity. He was allowed no visitors. No whisper reached him of the demands being made by ordinary people for mercy in his case. The people poured into the town from all over the country, and the military, fearing riots at the trial, posted extra guards and sent for reinforcements.

When the trial got under way, the court was surprised to receive a request from Miss Pugh of Lisgoole Abbey to speak on behalf of Proinnsias. She asked for a full pardon for him, and made it clear how impressed she had been with him as a gentleman.

'I am here, gentlemen,' she said, 'to ask this court to pardon Proinnsias Dubh. By way of compensation for all the robberies he is alleged to have committed, I would offer my whole fortune. He saved my honour, and I believe I owe him my very life.'

It was a very sincere and moving exhortation and Miss Pugh went on to speak at some length of Proinnsias' efforts to help the poor. She also offered to enter into any conditions the court might wish to impose, should they spare his life. She was listened to respectfully, but with no success.

Proinnsias was found guilty of robbing under arms, and the judge directed that he be publicly hanged outside the precincts of Enniskillen gaol.

When the day of the execution arrived, extra troops were posted around the site of the gallows. Even at this late stage, the authorities feared that a rescue attempt might be mounted.

Proinnsias made a long speech, in which he praised his men and thanked them for their friendship. He talked about the course his life had taken and the changes he would make if he could turn back the hands of time. He singled out Miss Pugh for particular praise in coming forward to speak on his behalf. When he had wished everyone goodbye he became silent. The hangman stepped forward, and as the gentle rain fell on the faces of the spectators, prayers were offered for the soul of Proinnsias. Moments later he was dead.

For a long time the crowd stood still, quietly staring at the body swinging on the gallows. The soldiers, muskets at the ready, tensed, waiting for some kind of outburst. The military commanders, having witnessed the execution, stood uneasily together, wanting to push through the mass of people, but afraid of a possible backlash.

In fact there was no retaliation. Everyone was stunned. It was as if everyone present had suffered a personal bereavement. Only slowly did the crowd melt away, silently and without any show of anger, their very silence an unnerving condemnation of the execution.

The body was later released to Proinnsias' family and the funeral cortège was taken by Lough Erne – few roads were truly passable in those days – to the wake in Bannagh. Following this ceremony, the remains of Proinnsias Dubh were buried in Carn outside Pettigo.

He is said to be the last man to hang on the old gibbet on Gallows Green, in the year 1782.

~4~

Cormacke Raver O'Murphy

IT IS SAID that places have a soul. Even when they become deserted and no longer used by man, the places retain their souls. The soul is kept alive through the memory and oral tradition of the general community. Songs, ballads and poems, together with the myths and legends are passed from generation to generation, until they become blurred with the truth and merge into the culture of the area.

Tories, rapparees and highwaymen are part of Ulster's culture.

Sadly, it is a much neglected part of our heritage. Only a few tories left a deep enough mark to be remembered. Scores, perhaps hundreds were buried in graves that are now lost and forgotten. Ulster has an inherent careless trait when it comes to its past. Only a few dates and events retain any significance and the people who were involved in those incidents are, very largely, ignored and unknown. The forests and mountains of this small province were once alive with men who accepted danger as part of their daily existence. They often lived off the land and had no interest in putting down roots; unaware that they were making any kind of history.

The forests and glens that grace Ulster now are smaller, quieter and softer than in the seventeenth century. Today the noises that disturb the peace of an evening are made by pigeons, starlings and blackbirds. Then, it was more likely to have been hard-riding men being chased by patrols, the clash of swords, and eventually, the crack of a gun.

Sir George Acheson, of the Gosford family wrote:

> ... the condition of the most part of Ulster is such as none dare travel or inhabit there, but as in an enemy's country – no trade, no work and no improvement....

He blamed the entire situation on the tories who, as far as he was concerned, were:

> ... against all industry and improvement, and all discourses and songs are in their praise, and they are accounted heroes.
>
> The embarrassed English gentry have them for dependants and purveyors – the common English living abroad in detachment fear them. Formerly robbed and went on their keeping; now they are in armed bands, and they force most part of the British to pay them yearly contributions, in paying of which, if they be negligent or not punctual, they presently come, rob the houses, drive the cattle into their retreats; that is in those mountainous and boggy and coarse lands inhabited only by the natives, whereof there are many in Ulster, and here they detain them till they pay much more than was at first demanded.
>
> These men thus terrify and discourage the British, having nothing certain but all at their mercy, they will induce them by degrees to leave those places of danger and recede into those more secure, which they daily begin now to do; and so, the lands will be laid waste, none else daring to take them, whereby the natives will rent them at such mean values as they please, and thereby embody themselves and grow numerous and opulent.

Sir George was a man of strong ideas. He it was who proposed a remedy that an officer with 'a party of troopers' be established 'with power to call upon any man to stand in the King's name and give an account of himself and shoot him if he don't; if he do, then try him by a jury on the spot, and if guilty to proceed to sentence and (after Christian preparation) hang him'.

Among other things, Sir George seemed to be under the impression that all tories had, as their only goal, the urge to drive the English out of Ulster. While this was true in many cases, and there were many tories who did see themselves as defenders of the poor, a great many of them were simply out to make money for themselves. It became a business, a way of life.

It would appear from the risks they took, and the life they chose to lead that many outlaws actually enjoyed their work. The option to give it up was open to them at all times. Looking back, it seems surprising, considering the difficulties they faced, that so many of them remained outlaws. The men were, in real terms, a very special kind of people with a great deal of courage.

Having courage, however, is not the same as having honour. The outlaws were not all honourable men. There were some who took from both sides, and there were some who fought amongst themselves for the leadership of the gang.

Such a man was Cormacke Raver O'Murphy.

Cormacke was the kind of man who, 'liked to run with the hare and hunt with the hounds'. For some time he managed to do just that – and quite successfully.

It was around the time that the parish priest of Killevy, Fr Murphy, was speaking out against Redmond O'Hanlon and his men, and advising the local people to refuse him shelter that Cormacke began to make a name for himself.

O'Hanlon had given the authorities many headaches over the years and was well established throughout the county. Support was widespread for the man many regarded as Ulster's Robin Hood.

In Fr Murphy's parish there lived a Lieutenant Henry Baker who employed Cormacke Raver O'Murphy. It was an exceptionally good position for Cormacke, as he was able to work for the Lieutenant and develop a lucrative sideline as as thief. He carried out several large robberies without arousing any suspicion that he had been involved in them.

The robberies were committed in various parts of Co. Armagh and Co. Louth, and Cormacke, being anxious to protect his reputation as a good law-abiding citizen was always at the front of any crowd complaining at what was termed, 'harassment of decent honest people'. He even managed to accompany the lieutenant to scenes of local robberies, offering his help as guide and intermediary between the irate tenants and the authorities. It was an excellent role he played for some time and could have continued without any risk to himself, had he not become too greedy.

Like any successful businessman, Cormacke was anxious to expand his operations. However, he made the mistake of allowing his greed to get in the way of caution. He entered a house one night while the tenants were out and helped himself to some of their possessions. He was unable to take them all away in one trip and, throwing good sense to the wind, returned a second time the same night to complete the job.

Unfortunately for him, the tenants arrived back before he had finished and he was recognised as he made his escape through a window. It is reasonable to assume that the occupation of his country, or striking a blow for freedom was not uppermost in his mind as he ran for his life. His sole desire was to stay alive and put plenty of space between himself and the military search party who were soon on his trail.

Tradition has it that his job with the lieutenant was filled by his brother William, and his uncle, Brian O'Murphy, got a job with the lieutenant's father-in-law.

Cormacke eventually managed to shake off his pursuers and remained in hiding in the woods. He had no food, no money and no weapons. With the patrols out searching for him, he could not return to his home and he knew that they would have searched his cottage and discovered other stolen goods. The choice open to him was either to become an outlaw, or to give himself up and dangle from the end of a rope.

He went on the road and for a time operated as a sort of freelance highwayman and robber. His victims often carried weapons which he confiscated as well as any valuables they carried. For a short period, life, if not comfortable or safe, was infinitely better than being dead.

He had not, however, bargained on retaliation from Redmond O'Hanlon, and soon found himself in trouble for stealing from people who were already under O'Hanlon's protection. Before long, Cormacke was 'arrested' by the outlaw's men and brought before the 'Count' to give an explanation of his actions.

It is easy to imagine the scene and how Cormacke must have felt at the time. There is no doubt he would have known all about 'Count' O'Hanlon and was probably terrified that he would soon dangle from a rope in the forest, or lose his head. The meeting would have taken place after dark, and Cormacke, blindfolded and very likely bound, would have been confronted by men around a campfire or in one of the 'Count''s many caves. The odd sword or knife might have glinted in the light of the fire whilst many questions were put to him. Lies would not have saved his life. These men knew what they were talking about and would not have accepted anything less than the truth.

It is not known what was actually said at the meeting. It is likely that O'Hanlon had already known Cormacke, and almost certain that he knew exactly what Cormacke had been doing since going on his keeping. It was not in O'Hanlon's nature to be rash, and he was reasonable enough to make allowances for the inexperienced Cormacke. Consequently, the outcome of the trial was that Cormacke joined the gang, probably after some initiation or swearing-in ceremony. It was easier to keep an eye on O'Murphy as a member of the gang, and to ensure that none of those paying protection money would be molested or robbed by a 'freelance'.

It did not take the enthusiastic Cormacke very long to establish himself in the gang and he soon progressed from being a part-time thief, to a full-time outlaw with a price on his head. He was now wanted by the authorities dead or alive.

Tradition suggests that Lieutenant Baker and Fr Murphy, acting on information received, came quite close to capturing the wily Cormacke. Each time, however, he eluded the search parties. They set several traps for him, ranging from messages that a pardon had been arranged for him, to offering negotiations leading to a pardon, should he surrender himself to their protection.

Being an enthusiastic officer, the lieutenant was in the habit of demanding results from all his patrols. On one occasion, a group of soldiers was so reluctant to return empty-handed to the barracks, that they rounded up several perfectly innocent men and women, on suspicion of having assisted the outlaw to escape. It may have placated the lieutenant but it was not the sort of public relations exercise that endeared the military to the local people. The lieutenant was caught in a difficult position trying to please his superiors and repair a fragile relationship with the community. Consequently, the need to capture Cormacke became something close to an obsession.

Cormacke had never had it so good. A strong forceful character, he got on well with the men and, while they found him a bit on the wild side, they found that they could trust him. He was certainly not without courage, and he proved himself to be a valuable member of the gang on several occasions and on numerous raids.

Things were going so well, that he might have submerged his identity into the O'Hanlon image, had it not been for his ambitious nature. One of the interesting traits common to most of the leading highwaymen was their ability, perhaps need, to be in control of events. We might never have known much about Cormacke if he had not believed that he would make a better leader than O'Hanlon and challenged him for the leadership of the gang.

The 'Count' had led his fifty strong gang for some time when Cormacke appeared on the scene. He had organised his men into small groups who could hit hard and quickly disappear into the hills. He had organised a timetable of reporting, sharing duties, distributing the proceeds of raids among the gang, and shaped them into a powerful effective force. It is difficult to believe that such a man had failed to guess the true nature of Cormacke.

Cormacke, to be fair, for a time remained loyal to

O'Hanlon. He led a group on O'Hanlon's behalf and was scrupulously honest in his work. However, having studied O'Hanlon's methods and style of leadership, he had convinced himself that it was time that the men had a new leader. It is difficult to accept that Cormacke had overestimated his own ability to take command, or that he lacked the essential qualities that would have brought him success. He was a capable enough man and had made friends in the gang. If he had succeeded in taking over from O'Hanlon, then he might have truly established himself as a difficult man to forget. As it turned out, he made one crucial mistake.

For years Cormacke had been loyal only to himself. Any decisions he made had affected only himself. He assumed that every man was the same. He did not take into consideration the loyalty to O'Hanlon of the other men.

On a windswept night in one of the caves near Slieve Gullion, he faced O'Hanlon across a blazing fire and challenged his leadership. It was a challenge neither man could afford to lose and could easily have resulted in death for either of them. Men moved immediately to O'Hanlon's side. They knew that, as their leader, he had to contend with such challenges. If he lost, they would no longer follow him. If he won, they would die for him. There was no compromise.

O'Hanlon also knew what was at stake and he had no intention of surrendering his authority.

'I took you into my ranks when you were alone,' he said. 'I gave you my trust and accepted you as a friend. I do not want to raise my sword against a friend.'

'Then you will die,' warned Cormacke, believing he was about to take command. 'You can no longer lead these men and you will either follow me or defend yourself.'

It was the rash, perhaps inevitable, challenge of a young

warrior, tired of taking orders, who genuinely believed his true position was leader of the pack.

It was then that O'Hanlon displayed the gentlemanly qualities for which he is remembered. He had no desire to kill his young opponent in cold blood, and no intention of ordering any of his men to kill on his behalf. He perhaps saw something of himself in the ambitious face of his young opponent.

'If we must fight,' he said, 'you will find me a willing adversary. However, these men appointed me their leader. I did not ask any of them to follow me. I respect their loyalty and their judgment. They have the power to change things. Let them decide who will lead them. I will accept their decision.'

Cormacke thought that he had won. Not all of the gang were present, but he felt sure that he had enough friends to side with him. In his eyes, O'Hanlon was a coward because he would not fight. The men would never follow a weak leader. The gang was his for the taking.

He was wrong.

They chose O'Hanlon. Cormacke was ordered to leave the cave and the protection of the gang. His life had been spared, but his pride had received a severe jolt. As he later made his solitary journey down the hill, he swore to avenge the humiliation. He was determined to make O'Hanlon's victory short-lived. He established himself as a highwayman again, and set out to rob victims under O'Hanlon's protection in an attempt to force the 'Count' into a fight. He began by robbing three Scotsmen who lived in the parish of Killevy under the protection of O'Hanlon. In charge of his own band of followers now, he had to prove to them that he was not afraid of anyone.

The three victims complained to O'Hanlon, who was less than pleased by the actions of his former friend. He immediately sent a party of fourteen men out to capture Cormacke. A short time later, his men returned with Cormacke and two of his supporters.

It would have been easy for O'Hanlon to execute the three men on the spot, and he may well have been expected to by his own men. Instead, he took the three prisoners to a safe house and sent for the three Scotsmen.

When they arrived, he handed the prisoners over to them with a note he himself had written to the next Justice of the Peace, identifying them as robbers. This would have meant certain death for the group and they immediately pleaded for mercy. O'Hanlon refused to change his mind and told them that their future was now in the hands of their victims. Cormacke and his men then began to negotiate with the Scotsmen and they, probably wishing to avoid any retaliation from the other members of the gang, agreed to accept £20 in payment from Cormacke, together with the return of their stolen goods. O'Hanlon reluctantly accepted their decision, but refused to return the weapons Cormacke and his men had been carrying when they were captured.

Cormacke had been made to look foolish in front of his own men and quickly set out to even the score with O'Hanlon. The fact that his life had been spared by O'Hanlon did not spark any flicker of conscience in his mind. Word had leaked out that there was no love lost between the two outlaws, and Lieutenant Baker, along with Fr Murphy, approached Cormacke with a plan to capture O'Hanlon. Under great secrecy they agreed to meet Cormacke outside the town and gave assurances that they would not inform the authorities of their rendezvous.

They offered Cormacke written protection from the law, and eventual pardon if he would set a trap for O'Hanlon. Cormacke was fairly certain that he could do the job and set about it with a great deal of enthusiasm.

He robbed a David Mulligan of Legacorry, who was also under the protection of O'Hanlon. Mr Mulligan protested through some friends to O'Hanlon, who sent a message to Cormacke demanding the immediate return of Mr Mulligan's goods.

Cormacke responded by saying that he would return the stolen goods if the weapons belonging to him and his men were returned. O'Hanlon agreed and a meeting was arranged between them. Cormacke informed the lieutenant who, in turn, arranged to have twelve soldiers dressed as civilians, make their way to the arranged meeting place and prepare an ambush for the tory.

In the meantime, the authorities took the unusual step of arresting relations of known outlaws, in an effort to obtain information about the outlaws, or at least, force outlaws out of hiding. Tradition claims that Mr Mulligan, on learning of the new steps, informed the military that he had been robbed, and the identity of the thief. Cormacke's brother was quickly arrested together with his wife, who, in order to obtain his release, admitted knowing where Cormacke had hidden Mr Mulligan's goods. The stolen property was recovered and her husband was released. O'Hanlon's informants told him what had taken place and he did not keep the appointment with Cormacke.

Cormacke was furious and blamed the army for ruining his plan, and threatened to ignore any future attempts by the lieutenant to capture O'Hanlon. The lieutenant, knowing his best chance was to remain on friendly terms with Cormacke, was profuse in his apologies and laid the blame for the breakdown in communication at the feet of his superior officers.

All this intrigue was carried on against a background of continued raids on settlers and the ambushing of travellers. Cormacke actually robbed a cousin of O'Hanlon, and on another occasion, after arranging through the lieutenant to keep the army out of the way, robbed a party of travellers in the hope that O'Hanlon would try to recover the property and consequently fall into a trap. The plan did not succeed because, again, O'Hanlon was warned of the plan by his informers, and stayed away from the area.

Cormacke O'Murphy was certainly persistent and refused to give up his attempts to replace O'Hanlon as the most wanted man in the county. He even tried to bribe O'Hanlon's men to leave the gang and join him. When they refused, he encouraged them to consider betraying O'Hanlon's whereabouts to the authorities and claim the reward.

It is doubtful if Cormacke ever seriously considered asking for a pardon. He still had the letter of protection from Lieutenant Baker and could use it if he were ever captured.

However, the lieutenant and Fr Murphy were putting a great deal of pressure on him to bring in the head of O'Hanlon. It has to be said that the priest was himself captured by outlaws and was in danger of losing his own head when Cormacke spoke on his behalf and persuaded them to release him. It was unusual for the outlaws to attack a priest, but they had all heard of Fr Murphy's condemnation of outlaws and considered him to be on the side of their enemy.

In what proved to be a final attempt to ambush O'Hanlon, Cormacke enlisted the help of an outlaw called Neale who sometimes rode with O'Hanlon. Neale's job was to find out what route would be taken by O'Hanlon on his return from a raid, and give the details to Cormacke. Sadly for Cormacke, Neale was a stranger to honesty and never subscribed to the creed of 'honour amongst thieves'. Despite having accepted money from Cormacke, he immediately revealed the whole plot to O'Hanlon who gave him £10 as a reward for the information.

O'Hanlon had been very patient with his former associate but there had now been several attempts on his life, all originating with Cormacke. He decided that it was time to put a stop to it. Accordingly, he let it be known that he intended to kill Cormacke at the first opportunity.

Despite his anger, it is unlikely that O'Hanlon would have killed Cormacke. He had only rarely resorted to violence and on this occasion he probably hoped that the threat of death would be enough to frighten the other outlaw into changing his attitude. He instructed Neale to give the word directly to Cormacke. Neale remained a few days with the gang before returning with the message to Cormacke.

Taking into consideration the influence O'Hanlon wielded throughout the county and the number of men under his command, the fact that Cormacke chose to ignore the warning is little short of amazing. He must have realised that O'Hanlon was quite capable of either killing him or putting him out of business.

However, Cormacke had spent so much energy trying to destroy O'Hanlon, that it was now his sole aim in life to succeed or die in the attempt. He responded to the threat by swearing that he would present O'Hanlon's head to the authorities. He followed this by attacking yet more settlers under the protection of O'Hanlon, and spread the word that the 'Count''s men were carrying out the raids. His actions became so outrageous that even Lieutenant Baker advised caution. This step may well have been on the grounds of self-interest. In reality, the lieutenant could exert only a limited influence on Cormacke, who now seemed to be beyond control, and who informed the lieutenant that he would make public his letter of protection. It was a situation that seemed to have no possible resolution. As it happened, it was resolved in a very unexpected manner.

Cormacke, as usual, had been relieving travellers of their valuables when, one night, he found himself to be running low on gunpowder. He contacted Neale and, through him, made arrangements to buy powder from a local contact. Alas, when the two men went to collect the gunpowder, Cormacke, who had consumed quite a lot of alcohol, became quarrelsome and they both launched into a bitter argument.

Cormacke pulled out his gun and threatened to shoot Neale, but Neale, the more sober of the two, also produced his gun. He did not threaten – he simply shot Cormacke dead. It was a tragic end to a man who had simply been too ambitious for his abilities.

Cormacke O'Murphy, despite his determination, never achieved his goal of leading the most powerful gang in Ulster. He is, however, the only man who seriously challenged O'Hanlon for the leadership.

A bizarre twist further emphasises the misfortune attached to Cormacke. Shortly after his death a few associates attempted to avenge his death by plotting to kill Neale. It was a total failure. Neale escaped and the would-be assassins were forced to go into hiding to avoid being put in gaol.

There is no record of Cormacke's grave. The recognition he craved never materialised and he is now barely even remembered.

~5~

Big Charley Carragher

FOLLOWING THE PLANTATION of Ulster, property in Co. Armagh was very insecure and travel decidedly dangerous. By 1612 Sir James Douglas and other settlers were regularly complaining that they were discouraged in their plantations by robberies committed upon them by the natives.

The Lord Deputy in his reply blamed the restless state of the country on the fact that the wooded lands offered shelter to such criminals, whom he called 'mischievous knaves implicated in the late rebellion and as yet unpardoned'.

He omitted to state that the lands these settlers were claiming as their own had been only a few years previously owned by the 'troublesome natives', or that any responsibility for the restless state of the country lay with the settlers.

Records of Armagh Assizes in 1615, reveal that the theft of horses, cows, oxen, sheep and pigs was very prevalent. Horses were then worth from about £2 to £4 each. Pigs, fifteen pence; sheep, twenty pence and cows, £2.

Anyone found guilty of such crimes was condemned to death by hanging on the public gallows which were situated on a spot called Gallows Hill. Public executions were carried out here for over two hundred years. The death sentence

was not confined to the theft of animals alone. Anyone convicted of stealing a portion of butter or a few eggs faced the
same sentence, although this was not always imposed.

The harsh judicial system existing in the seventeenth
century, may also be gauged from the sentence imposed on
four of the O'Neills.

Around the year 1623, the people of Armagh, not to
mention the authorities, were shocked by the kidnapping
outside the town boundary of Sir Benjamin Thornborough.
Four of the O'Neills carried Sir Benjamin into the woods
where they 'persuaded' him to write to the Lord Deputy
stating that he would be executed by his captors unless they
received pardons for past offences. The Lord Deputy was
not easily frightened and he proceeded to call their bluff. He
sent out patrols to hunt down the gang and, at the same
time, issued a statement declaring that unless the O'Neills
immediately released their victim, and surrendered themselves to his men, their families would face execution.

For a few days it seemed that a stalemate had been
reached with neither side prepared to give way. There had
been no sign of Sir Benjamin, and rumours were circulating
that arrests would soon be made. The local people were
wary lest they too would be involved in what was expected
to be a major exercise by the authorities.

It was the nerve of the O'Neills which gave way first.

Sir Benjamin was delivered safely into the hands of the
military, and his four captors were marched into Armagh
with halters around their necks.

It was assumed that they would be executed. Instead
however, the men were kept in prison for some weeks before being made to make a public submission on their knees.
They were then pardoned on the understanding that they

embark upon foreign service for a period of seven years.

The old prison consisted of a series of underground apartments directly under the Sessions House. A flight of steps led down to them, and from them, seems to have arisen the old Armagh adage; 'They will go down the nine steps', meaning that people would come to 'bad endings'.

Once Big Charley Carragher embarked on his career as an outlaw, there was no doubt that his end would be 'a bad one'. It was indeed to be a very gruesome affair.

Big Charley, or Cahal Mór as he was sometimes known, was a native of South Armagh. He made no attempt to follow in the traditional Irish Highwayman's footsteps. He had no hesitation in spilling blood, and terrorised the whole community. He first came into prominence as a local sheriff's bailiff, and was keeper of the Dorsey Pound where cattle were placed after they had been seized for rent arrears.

Shortly after his appointment to the position, Charley decided to launch into a sideline, namely, selling the impounded cattle to unscrupulous farmers and even more unscrupulous businessmen. It did not occur to him that the differences in numbers of those cattle seized and those still being held, would be noticed. He was making a tidy little sum out of his transactions and gave little thought to the possibility of being exposed. In real terms, of course, it was generally some time before peasant farmers could save enough money to reclaim their animal, and it is possible that he would have sold them an animal belonging to someone else, which would have probably kept them quiet.

His plan had very obvious limitations.

The discrepancy was eventually noticed and he was questioned about the disappearance of the animals. He denied having any connection with the alleged thefts and suggested that the animals had been stolen at night when he had been off duty, or when he had been away for a few minutes. The authorities were not totally convinced by his story. However, in the absence of any firm evidence, they allowed him to retain his position. They did point out that he might be held responsible for any future discrepancies.

Following this close shave with the law, Charley altered his tactics. Instead of selling the living animals, he began to slaughter them and sell portions. However, the authorities, not satisfied with his story about the missing animals, had arranged for him to be watched, and he was seen killing a cow. He was immediately dismissed from the post.

The position of pound keeper had been convenient and lucrative. Now Charley was out of work – and very angry. He was determined to get his revenge. While he planned his future actions, he began searching for other work and broke into houses while their owners were absent. For a time it was a rewarding occupation, and the work was not too demanding. He discovered that he had a talent for stealing.

Over the next few months, he kept a low profile. People saw him around the town, but few bothered with him. All the time, he was stealing ducks and hens to keep himself in food, and enough money to buy anything else that he needed. He was, of course, careful to spend very little of his stolen money in case his sudden wealth should be noticed.

As time progressed, however, he became careless, and a little too greedy. Until now he had been fairly careful in the choice of victim and had always selected those people who never varied their patterns of behaviour. On this occasion he had only watched the tenants for a short time before making his move. While he was robbing the house on the outskirts of the town one night, the owner returned and recognised him. He had no choice but to make a run for it, but only after having shot the man dead to avoid being captured.

Charley had suddenly graduated from being a small-time thief to a murderer.

On a bend of the old coach road leading from Dundalk to Omagh, not far from Lislea, there is a black craggy hill in the townland of Deburren and the parish of Lower Killevy. Close to the summit of the hill, lies a cave leading, they say, far back into the hills. It was in this natural fortress that Charley made his hide-out.

He cared little for planning and seemed generally to attack anything that attracted his attention. Before long the reputation of Big Charley Carragher had spread through the county. He was a brutal, short-tempered, powerfully built man, towering over six feet tall. If any foolhardy victim refused to give up his valuables, or tried to quarrel with the outlaw, Charley shot him.

Numerous military search parties spent days travelling back and forth across the county, following rumours and fading trails from east to west, north to south, through thick woods, up mountain slopes and along lonely paths over bogland hiding in the morning mists.

They would then return to barracks to learn that he had held up yet another traveller. Charley was finding that business was going very well. For the first time in his life he felt important and enjoyed his reputation. Soon he was attracting followers and had formed his own gang. They were all like Charley himself, coarse, reckless men who placed little value on human life and cared nothing for law and order.

When a man wanted to ride with Charley Carragher, he had to have committed at least one capital crime. Otherwise Charley would have nothing to do with him.

Sometimes the whole gang would swoop down from the hills on an isolated farmhouse. On other occasions, Charley would divide the gang into two factions and attack two targets at the same time. This was particularly frustrating for the military who were receiving conflicting reports of sightings from different parts of the county.

Charley had started his illegal career by stealing cows and horses, but now he decided to diversify his interests. He told his men to take anything on which they could lay their hands, and they obeyed his every command. Gold, silver, livestock, guns, ammunition, clothes. Even travellers who fully co-operated with the outlaws during a hold-up were sometimes shot or wounded, just to amuse the gang. There were times when individual members of the gang lashed out at the victim leaving him quite severely beaten, purely to indulge a desire to inflict injury and suffering.

The army, at this time, was having more than a little success in other areas. Sir William Steward of Co. Tyrone in a letter to the Earl of Arran on 13 February 1683 stated: '... we have reduced about thirteen Tories that were abroad in the county to one and a boy who keeps him company'.

Another letter from Sir William on 17 March 1683 claimed that he had very good hawks and hounds. And that he had '... equally good success in Tory hunting. In the last few days the last two of a gang of thirteen had been killed'.

On 2 January 1684, a letter to the Duke of Ormond's secretary describes the killing of Neal O'Donnelly and Hugh Duff O'Cahan, '... both whose heads we took off after some small dispute'.

Charley and his gang managed to elude the patrols for some time, but not without cost. One by one a member of the gang was killed or captured, and gradually the others decided to head for another part of the country. With no stronger bond than greed, it was only a matter of time before each felt the urge to go his own way.

As far as Charley was concerned, it meant that fewer people shared in the proceeds of any robberies. He remained immune to their departures. Before long, he was working on his own again.

Soon he would be dead.

Travellers in the area continued to be robbed, but now there were more who claimed that they had been physically attacked as well as robbed. It seemed at first that their stories were deliberately exaggerated in an effort to elicit more sympathy. But some of them had black eyes, bruises, and sometimes even broken noses – all allegedly inflicted by Charley. Their coats were almost always taken and were often later found torn and discarded some distance from the scene of the crime. It was puzzling for the military and a strange twist in the behaviour of the outlaw. Reports from victims often indicated that he hardly spoke to them while the robbery was taking place. They claimed that the silence made him even more frightening. He ignored their pleading to be allowed to keep their valuables, and appeared much more menacing if they pretended to have nothing worth stealing.

The military was under great pressure to capture Charley. However, informants failed to pinpoint his location. They were afraid that Charley might find out who had informed, and seek his revenge before being captured. It can be assumed that it was fear, not loyalty, that prevented usually reliable sources from turning up hard evidence.

One or two men did give some information to the army and were later found quite badly beaten and too frightened to identify their attacker. Even after Charley had called on houses, demanding food and sometimes shelter, the residents did not report him.

Unlike the situation with others in his profession, Charley's former position as a bailiff ensured that the authorities had an excellent description of him. Whereas many of his peers had commenced their careers as highwaymen when quite young, and later altered their appearance by growing a beard, Charley was a fully grown adult when he went on his keeping. Consequently, there was little he could do about his appearance that would confuse the troops.

He had made the mistake of living too long in the same place, and working too long as a bailiff to prevent some people from knowing at least a little about his favourite haunts. Some shebeens he preferred to others. Some fairs suited his particular talents more than others and, for whatever reason, he began to concentrate his attacks on a relatively small area.

It was with a great deal of patient information-gathering and much footslogging by the military that Charley was slowly forced into an even smaller area of work. He realised that they were squeezing him into a tiny pocket of land, and made several attempts to outwit them and head into a different part of the county. There was no way out of the ring of men looking for him. There were simply too many troops, and they saturated the whole of south Armagh.

Spies were planted in the markets and followed every man who even vaguely resembled Charley. The patrols were doubled on the roads between the fair towns. Travellers were directed to travel in groups for security. Military escorts were provided for even more groups of travellers. The roads, indeed even the spots where previous attacks had been carried out, were almost constantly occupied by soldiers.

It was the beginning of the end for Big Charley.

He had several encounters with the troops in his attempt to break out of the tightening ring of steel and redcoats. Each time, he failed and was forced to return to the safety of the hills. The army presence at fairs prevented him from selecting suitable victims. The increased number of soldiers on the roads reduced the time and safety margin at any robbery.

There was no peace for Charley. There were no longer any safe houses and no friends. He was totally alone.

His capture could be put down to his own bad luck; to the army's persistence; to their commanding officer's good luck; or to a combination of all three factors. It was on the main highway between Dundalk and Newtownhamilton while in the act of robbing a traveller that he was spotted by a patrol.

He made a run for it and managed to find a hiding place in the woods. For a time he thought that he was safe. He was wrong. This time the troops had a rough idea where he was hiding and continued to search the area. After almost three hours they found him concealed under a fallen tree. At first, he considered putting up a fight for it, but the sheer number of men in the patrol changed his mind and he surrendered without a struggle. They wasted no time in getting him to Armagh prison. His capture roused a great deal of interest and crowds of people headed for the town, anxious to catch a glimpse of the man who had terrorised the county for so long. Even at this late stage they expected him to make an attempt to escape, but there was to be no escape for him. If, when they finally saw him on the gallows, they had expected to see the same huge giant of a man whom they had once known, they were disappointed.

The months of being on the run from the military, and

the lack of good food and proper sleep had all taken their toll. The broad shoulders now sagged and the once huge frame had visibly shrunk. His massive girth had disappeared, and the clothes he wore all seemed much too large for him. His face was pale and drawn with wild eyes glaring out from under bushy eyebrows. Those who had known him before he had taken to the road were shocked at how weak his voice had become, and the effort it took for him to climb the steps to the gallows. He declined to make his peace with any god. Perhaps the fear in his eyes was caused by the prospect of having to face the ghosts of all those he had killed.

He was hanged, beheaded and quartered.

The court decided to make an example of Big Charley Carragher, and gibbeted portions of his body at the scenes of his worst crimes, as a warning to others who might be tempted to follow the same career.

It was his head that they set above the entrance to the cave at Cahal Mór's rock. Another quarter was gibbeted at Balls Mills. For a long time after his execution, people avoided these areas at night because of tales of ghosts and strange movement which, it was claimed, was the spirit of Big Charley fighting with the spirits of his victims.

It is doubtful if Charley made a huge amount of money out of his profession. There have been no tales of his 'buried treasure' or sackfuls of gold hidden under trees. It is far more likely that he squandered all of his takings. For a short time he was the topic of conversation round the fireplaces in every cottage in south Armagh. But the people had no respect for him. He brought disgrace to the profession of highwaymen. No time was wasted on writing ballads for Big Charley Carragher.

~6~

Toothless Shane from Tyrone

An outlawed man in a land forlorn
He scorned to turn and fly,
But kept the cause of freedom safe
In the mountains of Pomeroy.

ABOUT TWO MILES south-west of Pomeroy, and 900 feet above sea level, is a hill with the name 'Shane Bernagh's Sentry Box'. Who gave it this name is not known. But in the late seventeenth century Shane Bernagh Donnelly was a terror to the authorities.

His main hide-out was in Minyamer near the common border of Monaghan, Fermanagh and Tyrone. His activities were mostly concentrated between Dungannon, Omagh and Pomeroy. The name Shane Bernagh means 'Toothless Shane' and it is claimed that he never had any teeth, but so hard were his gums that he could bite through gold and silver coins, and even a tin plate, as easily as a piece of cheese.

Shane's real name was John Donnelly, or O'Donnelly and he was a scion of the ancient family of O'Donghaile, of Ballydonnelly, now called Castlecaulfield. His father, Patrick

Modardha (the Gloomy), had, during the 1641 rebellion, sacked Lord Charlemont's Castle. This castle occupied the site of the former fort of the O'Donnellys, who were of such high standing in native worth that they were the fosterers of the O'Neills. Proud Shane O'Neill was fostered there, and after a lifetime of battle, is reputed to have been buried on the hillside above Cushendun.

The O'Donnellys were dispossessed by King Charles II and this triggered off the oath of revenge by the clan. This was the cause of Shane Bernagh becoming a rapparee.

A considerable effort was being invested at this time by the authorities in their attempt to apprehend the rapparees. The rapparees for their part were doing their best to silence informers and discourage anyone who might be tempted by the reward money. Consequently, a lot of blood was shed throughout the province. Being an informer often resulted in having your tongue cut out. Sometimes the ears as well as the tongue were removed. In one court alone, in 1668, three rapparees were convicted and condemned for '… the barbarous and inhuman act of cutting a man's tongue out'. Other informers were often found hanging from a tree by the roadside. The authorities raised the reward money on occasions to £20 for the head of every rapparee. Captured outlaws were offered a pardon if they brought in the heads of two rapparees.

In a letter of July 1670 to the Government, Lord Donegal wrote that five of the most famous tories were killed or taken in the North: '… their names are MacGrath, MacGrote, MacLahannah, MacGuire and MacQuade. The first four were killed and had their heads cut off upon that place. The last is as tall as you ever saw and very well proportioned to his height. He could have escaped but was captured trying to save the life of his foster brother'.

Despite all this activity, it was admitted that a large number of tories were still very active in Co. Tyrone. The robberies continued and several people were murdered during August 1670.

For a time, Shane was a member of the gang led by Redmond O'Hanlon, but after O'Hanlon was murdered, about 1681, Shane went into business for himself. He became a popular figure with the local people and numerous ballads have survived about him and his peers which indicate his general standing in the community:

> Oh! call them not brigands, these chiefs in decay
> And weigh not their deeds in the scales of today.
> Let the children and gossips turn pale at the name,
> But just men to brave men give fairness and fame;
> Let us try them and test them, and shame us to be,
> If we still blame the name of the wrong'd Rapparee.

Shane was exceptionally good at stealing cows and horses and he was often compared to the great Cahil-na-Coppal in this field.

Cahil-na-Coppal, which means 'Charles of the Horse', was originally known as Charles Dempsey from Queen's County – the hereditary territory of the O'Dempseys. His father was a rapparee in King James' time, but took advantage of a pardon and settled down on a small farm.

At the age of twelve, Cahil was able to catch even the wildest colt, and was an expert rider. As he grew older, his influence over horses was so great that people believed that he used witchcraft to control them. He eventually became an outlaw and was a particularly efficient one.

He could neither read nor write, so he appointed his brother Daniel as his register and secretary. He kept excellent records of all the animals stolen and returned. When returning an animal to its owner after it had been stolen and a ransom agreed, he always charged a fee depending on the 'difficulty in finding it'. He hired assistants and spies in counties Monaghan, Leitrim and Derry.

When O'Hanlon was murdered, Shane left Armagh and took to the hills round Altmore where he ambushed travellers who journeyed from Dungannon to Omagh by the road used by King James II when on his way to Derry for the siege, and on nearby Protestant farmers.

From these hills he swooped down on his victims and disappeared again long before the military patrols could get anywhere near him. Descriptions of him vary, and it is difficult to be sure of accuracy. All the evidence agrees on the absence of teeth, and his skill with animals. He was also a man of exceptional strength and agility. Tradition claims that he could lift a fully grown horse, or knock a bull unconscious with a blow from his clenched fist.

When he stole cows or horses, he often concealed them in the caves and hills in the Altmore district where even yet the desertion of friends is known as 'leaving them in Shane Bernagh's stables'. He is also one of the first known rapparees to dye the horses that he stole, to prevent their identification.

He did not restrict himself to the stealing of animals and the occasional house.

Among those who suffered at his hands were Mr Evatt, High Sheriff of Monaghan in 1698, and a Mr Wright, a farmer from Emyvale. From both of these gentlemen he took a monthly fee – protection money – of £1, a quarter of beef and five stone of bread. If this was for his own consumption, it is amazing he managed to eat it all without the help of teeth.

A warning notice by the authorities in the Dungannon

area highlighted the growing menace of Shane's attention. It advised everyone in the community to be on their guard, and to lock up their livestock securely at night. It further claimed that:

> ... the Quaquers, the English, Scotch and Irish between Dungannon and Charlemont [had] been subjected to demands of tribute by the outlaw....

The announcement made no difference to Shane, who continued to raid and plunder wherever and whenever he pleased. Day or night made no difference to him. So dangerous had Shane become and so daring his raids that the Government decided to quarter in Altmore barracks a company of soldiers whose task was to capture him, dead or alive.

The first reference to military barracks at Altmore occurs in 1703. They were closed down in 1749 and quickly fell into decay.

The most memorable episode in the history of Altmore is its link with King James II who passed through on his way to Derry, accompanied by 12,000 men and a train of artillery. According to tradition, he journeyed through the village of Cappagh and watered his horse at the spring now known as the well of King James. On his way to Altmore, James spent the night in the ruined mansion of the Caulfield family, a castle destroyed in 1641, from which the modern village of Castlecaulfield derives its name, and from which the royal cavalcade set out from Altmore. Later, James turned southwards by the same route to his eventual defeat at the Boyne. At that time this road was the main highway from Dungannon to Omagh.

It was near here in 1806 that James Shiels was born. He was later to become a general, and governor of Oregon in the United States. He even challenged Abraham Lincoln to a duel, but the two men settled their differences without the use of pistols.

Isolated farms, travellers and coaches continued to be Shane's targets. He seemed to be everywhere at the same time. Sightings were reported in the east, west, south and north of the county. By now it was a matter of honour to the soldiers that the outlaw be captured. There were times when they got very close to capturing him, but luck had not been on their side. They were angry, tired men and they would not be getting any time off duty until the outlaw's head was spiked.

Shane was not unattractive to the ladies. He had a wife and a young son in one of his hide-outs, but his activities took him all over the county, and he would sometimes be away from his family for days at a time. He was rarely lonely.

Amongst his friends were a number of ladies who offered him a safe house and a warm bed. Because of his success as a highwayman, he was able to ensure that these ladies never went short of food or money. For their part, the women would also provide Shane with valuable information about the movement of troops and, sometimes, the routes to be taken by wealthy travellers. From a business point of view, both parties seem to have been well satisfied with the situation. If a few lines from an old ballad are to be accepted, Shane must have been a romantic figure in his time:

> 'Fear not, fear not, sweetheart,' he cried,
> 'Fear not the foe for me;
> No chain shall fall whate'er betide,
> On the arm which shall be free.

> So leave your kin and come with me,
> When the lark is in the sky;
> And it's with my gun I'll guard you,
> On the mountains of Pomeroy.'

It was the romantic streak in Shane that finally led to his death. Like many of his predecessors, Shane's courage at times gave way to recklessness and the taking of unnecessary risks. If he had curbed his impulsive nature, he might have avoided an early death and gone into retirement. On the other hand, without the courage and the recklessness and the romance, he would not have been the Shane Bernagh who dominated Co. Tyrone, and now lives in folklore and legend.

The commander of the troops in Altmore was, according to tradition, a man called Hamilton. He had earned the reputation of being a harsh, ruthless officer and was locally known as Black Jemmy Hamilton. He was, in fact, the sixth Earl of Abercorn, who had declined to accept the title and remained, Captain Hamilton. His loyalty originally was for King James, but he changed sides and became a staunch and loyal supporter of William of Orange. For his services to the Crown, he was eventually to become a general.

When stationed at Altmore, Black Jemmy was an ambitious officer. He knew that the capture of an outlaw with the reputation of Shane Bernagh would look well on his report and help in his attempts to gain promotion. Consequently, his men worked hard.

Every sighting of the rapparee was followed up and investigated. Every victim of the outlaw was visited and carefully questioned. Every coach load of passengers who had lost belongings was asked to provide detailed reports and descriptions of their assailant. Black Jemmy built up a wealth of detailed information on Shane, and his plan was to anticipate the outlaw's next move. Patrols were sent out to comb the hills, both night and day, but invariably returned empty handed and dispirited.

It was a time of narrow escapes for Shane, who was forced to stay well away from the cave where his wife and son were hiding. If the military had located his wife they would have used her as a hostage to force Shane into surrendering himself to them. In fact, what Shane did was to avoid any activities in the region of that particular hide-out and continue with his raids in order to lure the army away from her hiding place. He increased the attacks on farmhouses and travellers, becoming even more daring and foolhardy.

Black Jemmy was incensed at the continued freedom of the outlaw. His men were being constantly ordered to increase their efforts, and Jemmy himself rode out of Altmore barracks on several occasions, determined to bring back the outlaw's head. His luck was soon to change.

Shane was weary.

The patrols made it difficult for him to rest, and moving from one hiding place to another was highly dangerous. The troops were so numerous that any movement in daylight was almost certain to attract attention. Some of the soldiers had been ordered to remain close to isolated farmhouses to protect their owners and to cut off Shane's supply of food and shelter. It was a trying time for him as he watched the soldiers moving about the farms from his vantage points in the woods. He was desperate for food and supplies. He probably realised that it was only a matter of time before he was caught, but he was determined not to be taken easily.

There were times when he watched from the hills as the

troops rode out of Altmore Barracks, and one day he decided to take advantage of the situation.

Only a few men were left to look after the barracks during rapparee hunts, and it was an easy task for Shane to steal into the camp and help himself to fresh supplies and ammunition. It was an audacious and highly dangerous escapade. He knew the risks that he was taking and enjoyed the challenge. He also wanted to leave a sign behind to ensure that Black Jemmy would recognise the 'visitor' who had called during his absence.

As he was about to leave the barracks he was discovered by the young wife of an officer. She recognised him, but to his surprise, instead of raising the alarm, she engaged him in conversation about his exploits.

Being an officer's wife in the seventeenth century would not have been the most comfortable or interesting of positions The lady in question obviously found Shane Bernagh Donnelly more than a little interesting. Tradition has it that she became interested in the more intimate details of his life, and their conversation was continued in her bed.

When Black Jemmy returned, the lady claimed that Shane had forced his attention upon her. Consequently, more troops were brought in and the level of military activity increased. Among the hills bordering the Carrickmore–Omagh road the hunt continued without success. Then, acting on information received, the troops switched their attention to the slopes of Mullaghcarn Mountain.

There was no escape for the outlaw this time. The soldiers trapped him and there was a short gun battle. Shane ran out of ammunition. In desperation he used the buttons of his coat for bullets. In the end, he was shot dead.

> There's Mullaghcarn in feel and tarn,
> Its shadows cast in the moonlight lone,
> On the poteen dens in the fairy glens,
> That keep night vigils in fair Tyrone.

It was the end of an era in the county. Black Jemmy had succeeded in his mission and his men returned to Altmore Barracks, tired but victorious.

A number of versions exist about how Shane met his death. One claims that a follower betrayed him and he was shot in the face at Stramackilroy. Another states that a widow informed on him and he was captured in her house and beheaded. This report further states that his head was sent to the authorities for the reward money and his body was thrown into Loch an Albanaigh from where it was recovered by relatives. Yet another suggests that he was out hunting with his brother when the military trapped them, and Shane died trying to carry his wounded brother to safety.

Most, however, suggest that he was trapped and shot in a gun battle between himself and the army. Tradition claims that his brother brought word of his death to Shane's wife, and the woman, believing that the troops would come looking for her, took the drastic step of killing her infant son rather than let him fall into their hands. Before she could be stopped, she then stabbed herself to death. Part of the folklore about Shane records the last few moments of his wife's life:

> Foul Tory hunters, begotten in hell,
> Well may you raise now that dastardly yell;
> The eagle has fallen, but not in fair strife,
> And the heather is red with the stream of his life.
> The strong mountain eagle your false hands have slain;
> Alas! Ne'er to soar o'er the mountains again.
> Come cravens and see how the wild outlaw's wife,
> Will be true to her husband in death as in life.

~7~

The Costello Era

WHILE ONLY A FEW tories ever became truly famous, there were scores, if not hundreds, who might be called the 'nearly men'. It is impossible to gauge accurately the number of men who 'went on their keeping' for a short period, eventually giving it up to return to the quieter, safer, life of a peasant. Neither is it possible, because no accurate records exist, to estimate the numbers who styled themselves as highwaymen, who died in little quarrels or fights, who were no more highwaymen than the modern-day mugger.

However, there were some who did take on the forces of the military in a brief, though sometimes colourful struggle. They did not last for very long. These tories were incompetent or just plain unlucky enough to lack the necessary flair of their more illustrious peers.

Before they are totally forgotten, it is important that at least some of them should be mentioned, if only to avoid giving the impression that the profession was totally dominated by people like O'Hanlon, Donnelly, Crossagh and O'Haughan.

In the Newry area, a tory renowned as Anthony the Robber, certainly put fear into the hearts of travellers and tenants alike. He cared neither whether his victims were rich or poor, Irish or English. He had a simple philosophy.

If they had something that he wanted, he simply took it from them.

His methods lacked any finesse. A traveller would be stopped and threatened with death unless he emptied his pockets. It should have been a relatively simple choice. 'Your money or your life' is a statement that leaves little room for doubts or misinterpretations. A few, however, did try to reason with the tory, and paid the ultimate price for their courage.

Occasionally, Anthony would make an appearance at a local fair, and behind some stall or animal, he would quietly relieve a farmer of his money, before disappearing into the crowd again.

Some of his more popular fellow highwaymen were offered hospitality and shelter in 'safe houses'. Anthony the Robber was offered no such support. Consequently, he often obtained food and shelter at the point of a gun.

His last act was the murder and robbery of a young man called Willis Ryan who was returning from a fair. A few days after the killing, Anthony the Robber was seen and recognised on the outskirts of Newry. An immediate search was initiated by the military and he was eventually caught trying to steal a man's horse in order to effect his escape. He attempted to shoot it out with the army but ran out of ammunition and eventually surrendered. A few days later he was escorted to Downpatrick gaol where he was convicted with the minimum of delay, and executed on the gallows.

John Sallagh was labelled one of the 'worst Tories in the whole of Ireland'. For years he was the plague both of the community and the army. When he was eventually captured and safely placed in gaol to await his execution, everyone breathed a sigh of relief. John, not noted for his patience, decided not to wait for a court to hear his case and broke out of gaol. He returned to stealing cows and horses, but a few weeks later was again spotted by a patrol. He managed to escape without too much trouble and continued thumbing his nose at the authorities.

John was not a man to hide himself for too long. A month later he was seen at Mass and was approached by a local bailiff. There was a struggle during the service and the bailiff called for help from the congregation to overpower the tory. Those present at the service decided not to become involved in the fracas and paid no attention to the bailiff. John eventually gave up the struggle and found himself in gaol again, this time with shackles around his ankles.

It seemed to the authorities that he would cause them no further problem until the case could be brought before the court. They had seriously underestimated the strength of the desperate tory. He smashed his way out of the shackles and again escaped from gaol. This time he stayed out of sight, managing to remain free for a few months before he was yet again apprehended by the military and returned to gaol. Shackles and an armed guard ensured that there were no further escape attempts.

John struggled all the way to the gallows and died cursing his bad luck at being caught.

Neale Boy Milnatelle from Co. Armagh, if he could make contact with this world, would certainly claim to have been more than a little unlucky.

For a considerable time he had operated near Claudy and was doing quite nicely for himself until he robbed a William Acheson of some money and a sword. In the search that ensued, a crowd of about thirty people chased him across country, cornering him in the home of a friend in Ballylane.

They called upon him to surrender, but Milnatelle fired his pistol in their direction and the crowd scattered to the shelter of the trees. For a few hours there was a stalemate during which, some of the people began to lose interest in the hunt. None of them were willing to risk rushing the cottage in case they were shot. Two of the men had been sent to inform the military. However, with patrols out all over the country, the army was slow to respond to the request. Eventually the crowd began to melt away, arguing that they had not been robbed and no longer saw the point in hunting a man who had done them no harm.

As darkness approached, Milnatelle began to believe he would live to fight another day, and sat down with his friend to enjoy a meal. Those still remaining outside, rather than lose more face in front of their friends by returning home, decided at last to approach the house. The decision took some courage on their part as they were convinced that Milnatelle was well armed. In fact, he was completely out of ammunition and had only the stolen sword with which to defend himself.

It was then that his luck ran out.

Tradition has it that as the men approached the door, with the intention of breaking it down, the tory thrust his sword through a gap in the wood. The blade narrowly missed a man called Robert Lindsay, who instinctively retaliated by pushing his sword through the ill-fitting door. In an angry charge the men forced their way into the cottage, only to discover that Milnatelle had been killed by the blade of Lindsay's sword.

The authorities later decided that the killing was justifiable manslaughter, and no charges were brought against Mr Lindsay.

All four provinces of Ireland had their share of tories during this era. But Ulster seemed to be the most troublesome for the authorities. The Duke of Ormonde is alleged to have said that there were in Ulster, '... the worst Protestants and the worst Papists in Ireland'. Despite many years of tory hunting, the Government and settlers still did not seem to believe that they were in any way responsible for the situation, and concentrated their efforts on crushing the tories and imposing harsh punishments on those who attempted to oppose the new system of law and order.

It would be wrong to exclude the name of Dudley Costello from the names of Irish tories in the seventeenth century. Costello's origins lay in Co. Mayo.

He fought in the rebellion of 1641 and later served under Owen Roe O'Neill. He had a particularly colourful background. As Colonel Costello, he was among the garrison in Innishboffin that surrendered to Parliament forces in 1652. He retired to Flanders where he joined the King of England's colours. He became a captain in the Duke of York's Regiment, and distinguished himself at the siege of Betune.

On his return to Ireland, and failure to regain the family estate, he decided to earn his living as a highwayman. He was joined by a man with the name of Cornet Nangle.

At first they concentrated their efforts in Connaught, but the authorities there were so active and effective that the tories were barely able to make a living. They struggled on for a time, barely one step ahead of capture, moving from one hiding place to another, and striking at travellers on different roads. Luck was not on their side, and they were eventually forced to transfer their activities from Connaught to Ulster.

They settled in Tyrone, where, with little difficulty, they proceeded to launch themselves into business once more. The people of Tyrone displayed a more friendly disposition towards the two, and within a very short time, the outlaws established themselves as a successful team.

They did not have everything their own way, however, and continued to have many a close shave with the military. On one occasion, acting on information received, some troops rode into Fintona as dawn was breaking. They had been informed that Costello and Nangle were being sheltered by the inhabitants. The tip-off had been very accurate. The pair had spent the night in a safe house, but they were warned of the army's approach, and left without being seen.

Colonel Costello continued to operate in the area and was able to thumb his nose at the military. His own military training was of immense value to him and he had much greater experience than many of the soldiers who were working so hard to capture him. Because of his background he was able to anticipate their manoeuvres and responses, and consequently avoid their traps. Once he had familiarised himself with the terrain, he was able to move swiftly and confidently throughout the county. He proved to be very popular with the people, who were much impressed by his courtesy and good manners. The opinion of his unfortunate victims is a matter of conjecture.

The colonel had decided not to remain in the same part of the county for too long, despite numerous hide-outs and safe houses. By this time he was leading a band of followers, but insisted on operating in a guerilla-style fashion, thus making it very difficult for military intelligence to build up a pattern of his movements. He not only moved from one area to another, but also rode from one province to another. This meant that more than one commanding officer would be directing patrols to capture him, which often led to conflicting orders and duplication of patrols in the same areas.

When he felt that the military was getting too close in Ulster, he would return to Connaught and continue with his almost daily collections from unwary travellers. On one occasion, Lord Dillon, who was aware of the colonel's background, wrote to him advising him to give himself up and ask for a pardon.

Colonel Costello had already experienced the reliability of English promises and refused to surrender himself to the authorities. Being a gentleman and a soldier had not prevented him from being hunted like a wild animal. His service to the Crown had not given him back his lands. He valued his freedom, and fully realised how high the cost would be if he were ever captured. Nevertheless, he would not consider the possibility of surrender.

His resolve to continue his career as a tory may well have been strengthened by a proclamation on 25 June 1666 by the Lord Lieutenant. In essence, it demanded that Colonel Costello, Cornet Nangle, Christopher Hill, Thomas Plunkett, Charles MacCawel and their accomplices who, it claimed, were guilty of murder, burglary and robbery, lay down their arms before 17 July and submit themselves to the law of the land. It also imposed a price on their heads of £20 each. What probably angered the chivalrous colonel most of all was the offer to pardon any one of his men who brought in the head of any of his companions. Ever since forming his gang, Costello had made it clear to his men that they had volunteered to accept his orders. They were free to leave at any time. He particularly objected to the attempts of the authorities to turn one man against another.

Being named a traitor and outlaw meant that the colonel could be shot on sight, and he resolved to teach his enemies a lesson that they would not forget. He travelled with Nangle and no less than a hundred tories to attack a village where part of Lord Aungier's troop was quartered. It is difficult to imagine the scene from the vantage point of the twentieth century. However, in those days the landscape was very different and, provided men knew their way about, there was an abundance of hiding places. However, the actual organisation and direction needed to control one hundred individuals clearly indicates the quality of Costello's leadership. The movement of such a large body of men across country already full of soldiers is little short of incredible. It is possible that they moved about in small groups and later met at some agreed rendezvous before attacking their goal. Nevertheless, it clearly questions the efficiency of army patrols who would have been expected to locate at least some of the gang.

The fact is that the gang was not prevented from reaching its target, and the operation was a qualified success for Costello.

The tories burned most of the English houses and killed anyone who resisted. None of the Irish inhabitants was harmed, because of the planning of the colonel, who had issued very explicit instructions to his men. He had visited the townland a few days earlier and had carefully studied the best way to carry out the attack. His planning was superb. The tories suffered a few casualties, but inflicted substantial injuries to the troops who were completely surprised by the attack. When the outlaws finally withdrew from the scene they took with them thirty horses.

Unfortunately, Nangle was shot dead during the raid.

The colonel tried to rescue the body of his friend, but the military shooting was so fierce that he was forced to abandon his efforts and leave with the rest of his men. Nangle's head was cut from his body and sent to Dublin where it was spiked.

It was about this time that there was a mutiny in the garrison at Carrickfergus. The troops had not received any wages for some time and, despite pleas for money, they were completely ignored and took the only course of action open to them – mutiny. The Duke of Ormonde later recaptured the castle and court-martialled 110 men. Nine were executed for their part in the mutiny. It was decided to send the remainder of the men to the West Indies.

This was later changed when the men offered to pursue Colonel Costello in return for being allowed to remain in Ireland.

The general situation at the time was something akin to civil war. The years 1666–7 were particularly busy for both tories and military. The troops were combing the hills of Ulster for the outlaws with only limited success. At the same time, gangs of up to 100 tories were reported to be actively engaged in their profession throughout the country.

The sale of ale and beer dropped by a third because, it is claimed, people were afraid to leave the safety of their homes at night. Several tories were captured and hanged at the Easter assizes.

The name on everyone's lips, was Colonel Costello. He was one of the most wanted outlaws of the day.

He was back in Connaught again, warning the tenants on Lord Dillon's estates who occupied the former barony of

Costello, to leave or he would burn their crops. They decided that he was bluffing and refused to leave.

Their crops were burned.

The colonel regularly rode with about forty others and he then proceeded to burn the crops of the settlers in Castlemore, Ballylehane, Killmoore, Archville and Coyle Cashel. Despite almost frenetic military activity, the outlaws continued to plunder the settlers. It was as if the death of Nangle had driven Costello to the point where he was taking totally unnecessary risks – as though he had decided to seek revenge for the death of his companion. His men followed him blindly, oblivious of danger, ignoring the possibility of sudden death. The colonel's rage was to lead to his downfall and a major coup for the military.

He launched into a campaign of burning the settler's land along the banks of the river Moy, which had originally belonged to his family. Unknown to him, a large number of troops, who had moved into the area, arrived while a raid was taking place and, in a lengthy gun battle, he was shot and killed.

Without their leader, the rest of the gang fell into a panic and made a run for it. Some were almost immediately caught and executed on the spot. A few more died from their wounds and their bodies were found some distance from the scene of the battle. Those who escaped did not regroup and simply went their own way.

Colonel Costello's head was sent to Dublin where it was stuck on St James' Gate with his face towards his beloved Connaught.

By the year 1668 it was being claimed by the authorities that tories were being captured or surrendering every day. Part of the thinking behind this statement was to bolster the

flagging spirits of the foot soldiers who were spending every
day out in the hills, risking their lives to capture the outlaws.

The names of many of these highwaymen have now all
but disappeared, and only a few others lived long enough to
have proclamations issued against them. Patrick O'Son-
naghan was killed and beheaded in Co. Tyrone, Owen Mac-
Quire in Co. Fermanagh, and Donal O'Rortie and James
O'Loughnane in Enniskillen. The surviving tories struck
back at the military. Ambushes were set up to trap patrols.
Horses belonging to the army were stolen, along with weapons and ammunition. Barracks were attacked and the homes
of settlers burned. Domestic animals were taken for food.
For a time, the farmers of Tyrone were forced to seek refuge
in the towns because of the continued lawlessness. Only the
very foolish kept money in their homes.

The military continued their pursuit of the outlaws and
indeed had many notable successes. While it was officially
stated that the country was in a dangerous state of unrest, so
much so, that '... none dare travel except as in enemy country', the ordinary soldier continued to do his duty.

Sir George Acheson was a strong advocate of a continued campaign against the tories. He argued for more power
for the troops and demanded that every commanding officer
should be given the power to shoot anyone failing to give an
account of himself.

There were too many roving bands of tories in Ulster for
Acheson's policy to succeed. Many were caught, and at
every sitting of the assizes in the main towns of the province
whole batches of tories were tried and hanged, usually with
the minimum of formality. Sometimes the numbers waiting
to be executed were so great that only the leaders were
hanged, and the others deported.

On one occasion in Dungannon, 100 tories were in the dock. All were found guilty and ten were executed. The rest were deported.

An interesting outlaw of the eighteenth century was Séamus MacMurphy from Caledon in South Armagh. His ancestors had once been very powerful in the province but were eventually supplanted by the O'Neills from Tyrone.

Séamus was born in 1720, and tradition claims that he grew up to become a talented poet. Nevertheless, he made his living like any other highwayman of his time, taking what he wanted from the land and the pockets of the wealthy

He had two main weaknesses – drinking and womanising. One of his favourite shebeens was owned by a Paddy Daker – locally called Paddy of the Mountain. His premises was very well supported by thirsty highwaymen, and by Séamus in particular, who had a soft spot for Paddy's daughter, Molly.

The lady reciprocated Séamus' attention until she was told that he was being unfaithful to her with other women. Her father, with one eye on the £50 reward for Séamus, was quick to support his daughter in her condemnation of the tory. Together they arranged to betray him. It was an easy matter to get him drunk. By the time he awoke from his drunken sleep, Séamus was on his way to Armagh under heavy guard. It was the month of August, but for some reason he was not brought to trial until the following March. It was only a matter of selecting one of his crimes for the hearing, and he was condemned to death for the theft of a sheep.

Paddy and his daughter were mainly shunned by the local people for the betrayal of Séamus. The clientèle of highwaymen refused to drink in the shebeen and transferred their custom to another landlord. Tradition holds that it was one of Séamus' gang who actually hatched the plot for betraying Séamus, because he wanted Molly for himself. His scheming came to nothing, as Molly, so distressed at the outcome of the affair, threw herself into the river and drowned.

The literary skills of Séamus are claimed to have been immortalised in his poetic lament, written, it is said, as he was waiting to appear in court. There could be only one verdict and he was prepared to face it with dignity. However, his words reveal a more gentle side to his nature than is at first apparent:

> If I could only exist as a fern leaf in the sunshine on Ardaghy Hill, or on top of Fathom, or be a blackbird flying through Dunreavy Wood.

Séamus was executed on St Patrick's day in 1758. When he died, the winds of change were rapidly bringing the days of the rapparee to an end. The Battle of the Boyne was still relatively fresh in the minds of many people, and the rebellion of 1798 was already simmering. The first post chaise had been brought to Belfast, and meetings had already taken place in Belfast, at which it had been decided to raise enough money to build a poorhouse and hospital.

The rapparees were admired, despised, and feared. They were men of their era. Time for them was short and it was already leaving them behind.

After his execution, Séamus' body was taken to his mother's home in Carnally for the wake. He was later buried in Creggan.

~8~

Naoise O'Haughan

The Antrim Outlaw

NAOISE O'HAUGHAN, sometimes known as the 'Irish Robin Hood', was born of poor parents in the Valley of the Braid, near where St Patrick tended the flock of Milcha. To his friends he became known as Nessie, or Neeshy, and sometimes Ness, but he preferred to introduce himself as Ness O'Haughan, the Antrim Outlaw.

After the Battle of the Boyne in 1690 many Irishmen who had served with King James left the country and followed their calling as soldiers in other parts of Europe. Some, however, decided to remain in Ireland. A great number of the latter had once been wealthy landowners, and now found themselves dispossessed of their lands. Their skills lay with the sword and the pistol, so the obvious alternative to becoming peasants was to go on their keeping as outlaws.

There were proclamations against persons on their keeping, as well as against tories and rapparees, in the years 1696, 1697, 1698 and 1701. The first year of Queen Anne's reign was launched by a proclamation against those supporting tories, robbers and rapparees. Regular tory hunts were organised in attempts to impose law and order. But these were not always successful, and casualties on both sides were evenly divided.

An interesting fact emerges from the reading of old papers relating to the hunt for rapparees. They were almost always described by the authorities as brutal barbarians, and regarded by the local people as heroes. In a letter from a gentleman in Armagh, dated 17 July 1697, there is a description of the brutal treatment of a prisoner held by tories. The army had been searching the hills for some time for a particular group of outlaws and, after catching up with them, there was a gun battle which lasted for most of an hour. The gang then broke up and made a run for it. According to the writer of the letter, when the army entered the camp, they found the body of a colleague, Captain Groves, who had earlier been taken prisoner by the outlaws. He claims:

> ... one of the rogues had driven his bayonet into the heart of Captain Groves, and then rowled it round in his body until he had expired....

The seventeenth century was, it seems, not only a time for brave men, but also strong stomachs. The heads of the tories who died in the gun battle were taken into town and spiked on the wall of the Sessions House. This gruesome habit was widespread throughout the country. During the sixteenth and seventeenth centuries, the spikes on the gaol walls at Carrickfergus, Armagh, Derry, Downpatrick and Dundalk were constantly being replenished.

It was into these violent troubled days that Naoise O'Haughan was born around the year 1691. One of four sons, his parents were poor farmers and had a small plot of land north of Slemish in Co. Antrim. The boys and their foster brother, Philemy, spent much of their time poaching to help supplement the family diet, and cock fighting.

Life was difficult, but Mrs O'Haughan had ambitions for her sons. She was a realist, who knew of only one way in which they could escape from the back-breaking, grinding poverty that she had experienced throughout her life.

They would have to become highwaymen.

The parents launched into a rigorous Spartan training programme, where the emphasis was on fleetness of foot and general agility.

One exercise of which they are said to have been fond was to open the two doors of the barn, each parent taking up position inside one of the doors, one on each side, armed with a flail with which they struck the floor alternately. The children then had to run in at one door and out at the other end without being hit by a flail. The boy who was most nimble obviously received the fewest knocks and bruises.

The boys earned a reputation for their agility, and Ness in particular was highly regarded for his jumping ability.

For a time, as was the custom, Ness was fostered with another family, and it was here that he learned how to use a pistol and a sword, becoming something of a crack shot.

About the time he was due to return home again, the barley rent was doubled for smallholders. Like many other families, the O'Haughans found it impossible to pay the extra. The bailiffs were sent in to evict them and, during the subsequent fight, Ness killed one of them with an axe.

Mrs O'Haughan, being the more daring of the two parents, said that it had been a sign from the Almighty himself that it was time for the boys to make their way in life. And so, the O'Haughan brothers, Ness, Shane Oge, and Roger, went on the run, along with their foster brother, Philemy.

It was a ready-made gang – the beginning of a legend.

For a time they operated in the districts of Glenwherry and Ballyboley. They had caves in several places where they were safe from search parties. It goes without saying that the caves became known as O'Haughans' Caves, and the name eventually found its way onto the modern survey maps. In the interests of safety, the gang had many other hiding places – Magherabawn, King's Moss near Ballyclare, and a spot known as 'Archy's Bushes' on Knockagh mountain. This last hide-out was close to the residence of one James McKinstry who frequently gave them hospitality in return for immunity from possible robbery. Then there was a Widow Jacques, whose home they used on occasion. Although the authorities were ruthless in their treatment of anyone suspected of supporting the outlaws, many of the local people remained loyal to the O'Haughans until their death.

The youngest brother, Denis, had always shown little enthusiasm for becoming an outlaw. However, he succumbed to parental pressure and joined the rest of his brothers. His lack of enthusiasm was well founded because he did not survive very long as a highwayman. Shortly after the boys set themselves up in business, they carried out a robbery on Carrickfergus Common. Denis took a fancy to the clothes of one of the victims, and demanded them. A few days later, he was seen wearing the clothes as he entered the town, and was identified by John MacDowell and William Purtavens.

The two men quickly informed the military and Denis was arrested, tried and executed. The informants were given £10 reward for being good citizens. According to tradition, the other brothers watched from the safety of the crowd as the execution took place.

Ness had many friends in the local community, and to these he remained completely loyal. In general terms, he concentrated his activities on the rich members of society, although this was not exclusive. As far as he was concerned, business was business. He frequently gave money to the poor, however, possibly by way of insurance.

Shane Oge O'Haughan married Jean McKinstry from Carrickfergus. It was through her that he was captured. There had never been any love lost between Shane Oge and his brother-in-law, Séamus Bawn McKinstry, and the relationship developed into one of pure hatred.

McKinstry, having placed men in a ring around the cave where he knew Shane Oge was hiding, informed him that his wife Jean was seriously ill and not expected to live. Assuming that he was hearing the truth, Shane Oge decided to go with McKinstry to Carrickfergus. Ness, who had also been in the cave, offered to accompany him. As they left the cave, McKinstry's men attacked them.

After a lengthy sword fight, Ness managed to escape. Shane Oge was marched into town where he was tried and executed with the minimum of delay. McKinstry received £10 for his part in the affair. John Edmonston, William Craig and Daniel McKent each got £3. Robert Allen of the Braid got £5, and a further £12 was divided between Samuel, Robert and Hugh Beggs.

McKinstry's actions resulted in his becoming an outcast in the local community, where the O'Haughans were held in a great deal of respect. After collecting his reward, he moved to the Braid for his own safety. Rumours were already circulating that the O'Haughans were out to kill him. Moreover, he received a number of beatings from former friends who had also voiced hints that he should be shot. Had he not been a brother-in-law of the dead man he might have remained in the community. He was a thatcher by trade, but because the people of the Braid shunned him he could not get any work and eventually died alone and in poverty. His own family did not even attend his funeral.

Ness and the remainder of his gang joined forces with another band of outlaws led by 'Captain' McAllister who operated an area from Buckna to Carrickfergus. The men were tough, hard-riding characters with no regard for danger or the rule of law. They had no hesitation in using violence to achieve their ends, and Ness disliked their methods. Nevertheless, there was safety in numbers, and he agreed to go along with them for a time. When the 'Captain' was captured and hanged, the O'Haughans took control of the entire gang and refused to allow anyone to use violence towards their victims. 'O'Haughans' Cave' at Ballyboley became their base at this time, but after its location was discovered they moved to the Collin near Ballyclare.

The waylaying of hundreds of victims travelling through Templepatrick on their way to Belfast continued. No one was safe. With poor roads and lack of good communication, thick glens and fast-flowing rivers with which to contend, the military were no match for the gang. However, they maintained the pressure. Tenants of small cottages and farms were constantly being disturbed during the night by troops demanding to search the premises.

Ness and his gang were again forced to move headquarters, this time closer to Carrickfergus. Their reputation was known far and wide and they feared that someone would betray their whereabouts for the reward money. The raids, however, continued unabated.

The gang went on a great plundering foray in the valley of the Braid, taking by force anything they fancied, and levying blackmail all around. Rather than lose their homes or stock, the people paid the protection money. On their way back from the expedition, the gang stopped for drinks in an isolated shebeen. While they rested, the place was surrounded by local tory hunters and a military patrol.

In the ensuing battle, most of the members of the gang were killed or wounded. Ness only just managed to escape by pretending that he was dead and hiding under the bodies of his dead companions. As the army began moving out with its prisoners, the tory hunters moved in to take the heads of the dead outlaws. That was when Ness made his move. He jumped to his feet and threatened to shoot the first man who moved or raised the alarm. One man, 'Singing Robin Allen', was foolish enough to make some kind of move. It startled the nervous Ness who fired his gun. In all probability he meant to kill Allen, but pistols in those days were not noted for their reliability or accuracy. All that Allen lost was part of an ear and, no doubt, a lot of blood.

The following remnant of an old ballad gives a more colourful description of the battle:

> The bold Nessie O'Haughan
> And Shane Oge the Tory;
> Little Owen Murphy and
> His younger brother Rory;
> Randal Dhu Agnew,
> McKinstry and Magennis,
> Though half the Braid pursue
> Make good the Upper Teenies.
>
> The last man in the rere
> Had barely cleared the clachan,
> When a bullet grazed his hair,
> 'Twas burly Nessie O'Haughan,
> 'Stand, comrades, now,' he cried.
> 'Why flee in such a hurry?
> Let's tame the Begg's pride,
> And cave the Craigs O'Skerry.

'Range round your chief, my men,
These are but shabby fellows;
Ere we swing upon the gallows.'
With that whizzed through the air
A bullet from the caller,
Which carried off the ear
Of 'Singin' Robin Allen'.

John McCrea of Ballynure later received a reward of £5 for the capture of Randal Dhu Agnew, mentioned in the ballad, and Agnew was executed at the Gallows Green, Carrickfergus in 1717, convicted of breaking into the house of a farmer. Two other outlaws, Rory Murphy and Toal Magennis, fled the country in order to avoid the same fate. The gang was now in danger of falling apart despite the efforts of Ness. He eventually decided that they should all go their own ways, and only his two brothers remained with him.

Philemy and Roger were captured and executed in 1718.

Ness was alone.

There were some who did not share the country people's admiration for the outlaws. These were tough experienced men who made a living out of hunting and killing them. They had their reputation as tory hunters to protect, and mercy played no part in their profession. The most notable of these early bounty hunters was Johnny Johnston.

According to Lord Ferrad's letter of May 1729:

My Lords,
Since I first had the honour of recommending the bearer John Johnston to the Government, I have never had a blush on my face for his performance. He has cleared the roads to Armagh and all neighbouring counties so well of the rogues that used to infest the country that he has rendered the roads passable....

According to assize records of Co. Antrim, Mr Johnston is listed as having been voted various sums of money by the

Grand Jury of that county, between the years 1716 and 1739.

Tradition has it that his executioner-in-chief was a man named Keenan, known in Irish as 'Caonan na gCeann' – Keenan of the Heads. Keenan had so many decapitations to his credit – one hundred and ten – that it is no wonder that he was less than popular with the fraternity of highwaymen.

One of the remarkable facts about Ness is the reputation he gained as a 'gentleman outlaw'. After all this time it is impossible to state exactly where the legend ends and truth begins, but his 'gentleman' tag does persist, suggesting some truth in it. Travellers used the roads after dark at great peril to their valuables, but many claim how impressed they were at the manners and courtesy displayed by the outlaw.

He was a powerfully built man with a quick laugh. Some of his victims described him as a very handsome man and 'very becoming, in his feathered hat, blue French side-coat, with silver buttons and lace and red waistcoat'.

Despite his claim that he had never killed anyone, there was a reward for his capture, dead or alive.

The price on his head which had started as £5 – four months' wages in those days – rose to £20. The official desig-nation by the authorities of 'Outlaw' meant that he could be shot on sight by anyone, with the full support of the law. By now, pursuit was almost continuous, with tory hunters combing the hills for him. His thick black hair was already turning grey, and he was only twenty-three years of age. His friends grew even more worried. Ness would simply shrug off their concern and tell them, 'One day they will take me. But I will surely leave them with a story'.

To his allies he was now particularly generous. He re-paid the support of isolated homes with food, usually stolen from the more wealthy, and money, always taken from the rich. Tradition claims that a friendly farmer was to be evicted because he had not paid the rent, and Ness gave him the money to clear the debt. Ness later recovered the money by taking it from the land agent.

An old man called Alison openly supported Ness for a number of years. On occasion, he gave him food, and they shared a friendly relationship. When in the area, Ness would tie a few guineas in a rag and hang them on the door-latch.

He also had a conscience. One Sunday night he was about to rob the house of a man by the name of Gilmore, near Roughfort. On hearing the family singing psalms, he changed his mind about robbing them, apparently deciding that they were better employed than himself.

Operating alone meant that Ness had to rely entirely on his own skill and resources. There were no lookouts, no extra eyes, no one to prevent him from being shot in the back.

Several times he only narrowly avoided capture. On at least one occasion, the speed and agility he had learned as a boy saved his life. A military search party surprised him one day while he was separated from his horse, and his only option was to make a run for it. The soldiers gave chase. He tried to throw them off his track by hiding and doubling back on himself, but didn't succeed. They began closing in on him, apparently having decided to take him alive. Only a few shots were fired in his direction.

Ness was no longer as fit as he had once been and the spring had left his legs. Sheer desperation kept him going and helped him ignore the pounding of his head and the burning in his throat. Still the soldiers came after him. Knowing the land better than they did, he managed to keep ahead of them until he passed Divis and crossed the Bog Meadows. With a supreme effort, he raced down the hill, jumped across a deep, but relatively narrow, stretch of the River Lagan and hid in long grass on the Co. Down side. An old man who was ploughing close to the spot denied having seen Ness when the military arrived and questioned him.

Having searched the area for some time, the soldiers went off in another direction. The ploughman provided Ness with shelter for the night. During their conversation, he said that he had never seen such a jump in his whole life.

'That may be,' said Ness. 'But don't forget I had a ten mile run at it.'

Ness, when running from another search party, injured himself by clearing the Deer Leap on Lord Antrim's estate. He had to lie low for several days after that and then moved to a new hiding place. This time to Ballytoag in the hills north of Belfast. Here, he operated from the safety of a friend's farm who lived near the Hanging Thorn, beside the Catcarn and between McIlwhan's and Squire's Hill.

His most spectacular hold-up took place on the Lammas fair day of Belfast. He positioned himself close to Ligoniel and as each traveller from the townlands of Ballynabarnish, Templepatrick and Antrim made his way towards Belfast, he was seized and robbed. Each victim was then securely tied, gagged and held in a spot called 'O'Haughan's Hove' or the 'Pedlar's Grave', close to what is now the Crumlin Road. At the end of the day, he had twenty hostages. The total amount stolen from them is not recorded.

As darkness began to fall, he untied one of the hostages and left with instructions that the man should untie the others and let them get home in case it started to rain.

The local people were beginning to regard the outlaw as some kind of superman. His exploits found their way into the poems and ballads of the day. No doubt these were embroidered into very tall stories around many cottage fires.

> Of a very fearless highwayman
> A story I will tell.
> His name was Naoise O'Haughan,
> In Ireland he did dwell.
> And on the Antrim mountains he
> Commenced his wild career,
> Where many a wealthy gentleman
> Before him shook with fear.
>
> A brace of loaded pistols,
> He carried night and day,
> He never robbed a poor man
> Upon the king's highway.
> But when he'd taken from the rich
> Like Turpin and Black Bess,
> He always did divide them with
> The widow in distress.

The military had no such illusions about Ness. He had made them look foolish on a number of occasions. They faced the same problem that handicapped many of their colleagues in hunts for rapparees. They did not know the country well enough and they underestimated the ability of the outlaws to use the natural cover of the land.

Ulster looked very different in those days. There were great forests and bogs and parks and wolves. A great park stretched from close to the centre of Belfast as we know it now, out to Stranmillis, was stocked with deer and used by the wealthy for hunting and hawking.

The weary soldiers who searched in vain were almost ready to believe that Ness O'Haughan was a ghost. Reported sightings were received from all over the county. Frightened travellers, even when they had not been robbed, were ready to swear they had seen the outlaw on their journey.

For the last few months of 1719, Ness continued to take

donations from the well-heeled travellers. The entire area around Divis, Squire's Hill and Cave Hill was avoided by all but the most foolhardy traveller. Even well-armed stage coaches often found their way blocked by the dark figure on horseback with a brace of pistols. Beyond the reach of the military, he remained the charming highwayman who, with much panache, introduced himself as the 'Antrim Outlaw'.

However, those who knew him saw the changes.

He laughed less and seemed to prefer his own company to that of his friends. He was seen less and less on the roads. Rumours began to circulate that he had left the area. Some even whispered that he had been shot or captured. The more imaginative travellers claimed to have seen a riderless black horse on the hills as they returned from the fairs.

Ness was not dead. Yet he was no longer molesting travellers and merchants; and the coaches arrived safely at their destination without any mishap. Why?

Any explanation must be guesswork. The hills were full of soldiers looking for him. The tory hunters were still determined to claim the reward for his head. The local merchants and businessmen wanted to see him locked up in gaol. Put these together and it would be easy to claim that things were too hot for him and he was simply lying low. He may even have left the area for a while. It is recorded in a history of Co. Louth, far from O'Haughan's native soil, that a reward was paid to two tory hunters for the head of the '… noted Tory and Rapparee, Eneas O'Haughan….'

There is another possibility. For most of his life he had been forced to move from one hiding place to another like a hunted animal. There was a guard on his home and he had not seen his family for a long time. The men who had followed him were dead or out of the country. He had seen his brothers die at the end of a rope. Alone with only the sound of the wind in the trees for company, and the emptiness of the lonely hills for a home, he may simply have grown tired.

Then he made an extraordinary decision.

In an attempt to 'disappear' completely, he joined the army under an assumed name. In the company of other men he was happy again and it seemed that he really had escaped from his reputation. However, there was to be no escape for Ness O'Haughan.

At an army sports day competition he saw the chance to make some easy money by accepting a challenge to out-jump his colleagues. The bet was to jump over four horses standing side by side. He cleared it with so much ease that it raised comparisons with the agility of the Irish rapparee O'Haughan. He was closely questioned as to his origins and would have got away with the ruse had it not been for the good memory and sharp eye of an officer. Ness had been so minutely described in the proclamations issued against him that a birthmark proved his true identity.

There was no point in further deceit and Ness confessed.

Within days he was taken under military escort to Carrickfergus where he was tried and condemned to death. For giving evidence against him, and so proving his guilt, £5 was paid to John Hawkins and £15 to Daniel Philips of Ballymascanlon. According to the record books of Carrickfergus, the year was 1720.

Over the years, Ness was believed to have accrued a considerable fortune. His brothers were all dead and his family under arrest by the military. Ness, anxious to help his parents and younger members of the family, made a request to speak to a friend – a Mr Johnston from Ballytoag – and asked him to see that his parents got the money.

He told Johnston:

'If you go to the Carn Hill, beside the Hanging Thorn you'll find a box of money buried beneath a spot from where you can see five castles, five loughs and five counties. If you take five jumps to the east of that spot, you'll find a skin of gold.'

The Hanging Thorn was so called because someone had committed suicide by hanging themselves on it. Consequently, it became a place to be shunned.

Mr Johnston did not wait to see the execution. He immediately galloped off and made his way along what is now the Shore Road and turned up the highway where the Throne Hospital was later built, to the Cave Hill and the Hanging Thorn. He found a box of money, but the gold has not yet been discovered.

Ness continued to be polite and cheerful as he climbed the gallows. He wished everyone goodbye and thanked them for their attendance as the rope was placed around his neck.

He and six other 'notorious malefactors' were hanged at the same time at Gallows Green, Carrickfergus. Their heads were later spiked on the top of the courthouse. By coincidence, Ness' head was spiked beside the bleached skull of his brother, Shane Oge.

On a more ghoulish note, tradition claims that, shortly after the head of Shane Oge had been spiked, an eagle tore his eyes out, and about a year later, a wren built a nest inside the skull. Some months after Ness was executed, his skull was blown down in a strong wind and crashed through the window of a nearby schoolhouse. The schoolmaster is reported to have placed the skull on his desk in full view of the pupils to ensure that they remained attentive.

~9~

'Count' Redmond O'Hanlon

A shepherd who lived on Slieve Gullion
Came down to the County Tyrone,
And told us how Redmond O'Hanlon
Won't let the rich Saxon alone.
He rides over moorland and mountain
By night till a stranger is found,
Saying, 'Take your own choice to be lodging,
Right over or under the ground'.

DURING THE SEVENTEENTH and eighteenth centuries there were hundreds of rapparees operating throughout Ireland. Some, like candles, flickered into prominence for a short time; a few achieved lasting notoriety in both folklore and ballad. Towering above them all, was one who dominated the scene for over twenty years. So well known was this man, and so popular with the people, that Sir Walter Scott declared it his intention to base a book on his exploits. Alas, the book was never written, and it was left to the people of Ulster to immortalise 'Count' Redmond O'Hanlon.

The clan Hanlon was settled at Orier, Co. Armagh, their chief being hereditary standard bearer, north of the Boyne. For loyal service against Hugh O'Neill, Earl of Tyrone, the then reigning chieftain, Oghie O'Hanlon was knighted by

Queen Elizabeth, and received a grant of all the lands held by the clan for his life with succession to his sons, and failing their heirs, to his brothers. However, following the rebellion of 1641, the English Parliament ordered that all Roman Catholic landowners of Ulster be removed to Connaught.

Redmond O'Hanlon arrived into the world near Poyntz Pass in 1640. He was educated at an English school and displayed both a complete mastery of the language, and a talent for mimicry, which was to be of use to him in later life.

Little is known about his early childhood, but as a young man he was present when a man was killed in a quarrel, and to avoid being arrested, travelled to France. He stayed there for some time, and it is thought that he served for a period in the French army. He refused to return to England for the trial, and was outlawed. He consequently returned to Ireland, fluent in both French and English as well as Irish, and fought under Owen Roe's command at Benburb.

It was not long before the young O'Hanlon established himself as a rapparee in Ulster, and within a few months he had gathered a band of over fifty followers. It was then that he used his military experience and training to devastating effect. He had a natural flair for leadership. Unlike many of his peers and predecessors, O'Hanlon did not insist on operations being carried out by one huge gang. He knew that it was impossible to feed, clothe and satisfy such a band, and realised the difficulties in moving such a force across country in secrecy.

What he did was to organise his followers into companies, each with its own chosen leader. He then gave each group a designated area in which to work, while he remained in supreme command. It was a brilliant scheme. For the next twenty years, O'Hanlon and his gangs controlled three counties: Armagh, Down and Tyrone. He soon became so famous that every robbery committed was attributed to him. By then, anyone whose name was presented as a tory by the Grand Juries of the counties, and proclaimed as such by the Lord Lieutenant and Council, could be shot as an outlaw and traitor, without trial.

It is a tribute to O'Hanlon's skill and charisma that so many chose to follow him. Amongst the better known members of his gang were Strong John MacPherson, Shane Bernagh, John Mulhone, James Garreck, Harry Donoghen, the Napper and Patrick MacTighe. Many of his relations also rode with him, including his brothers Edmund and Loughlin. Loughlin was later killed by a John Mullin, who received £50 reward for killing the outlaw. Redmond had many hiding places, including at least one souterrain.

His organisation skills were quite extraordinary for the time. With such a large band of followers, he imposed his will throughout the territory, and soon no one dared travel, except in convoy, without his personal pass.

Tradition claims that it was the custom for the country folk to pay the outlaws for a pass to travel unmolested. There is no doubt that roads all over the country were unsafe. Even when travellers had nothing of value with them they were glad to fall in with others going the same way, not only for company but also for mutual protection. But even this was of little help in the more remote parts of the counties, if they encountered one of the larger bands of outlaws.

So large were these bands that one party consisted of 28 horsemen and 20 on foot. The ordinary peaceful citizen had every right to be frightened, as the dangers he faced were by no means imaginary.

If any locals were even suspected of giving information

to the military, they ran a very real risk of having their homes burned down. It was claimed that some informants had their ears cropped, or their tongues cut out and '... sometimes they were kept prisoners for whole nights stark naked in the open fields'.

O'Hanlon's regulations at least ensured some element of fair play. He levied a fee of two shillings and six pence per year from every farmer, but guaranteed that they would not be robbed by any of his followers. His men were supplied with lists of all the people under his protection, and given strict orders not to meddle with such persons or their goods.

O'Hanlon, known by his men as 'Captain', was a man of his word.

On one occasion he deliberately had a man delivered to Armagh gaol who had robbed a pedlar in his name. It was savage retribution. O'Hanlon knew that the man would be executed at the next assizes for theft, and his head spiked on the Sessions House. To ensure the man's conviction, O'Hanlon had obtained a signed statement from the victim of the robbery and had it delivered with the unfortunate outlaw.

Meanwhile, the gang continued on its way, robbing travellers and coaches, and collecting protection money. Even though the smaller groups did not see their leader every day, they still carried out his orders and reported to him every six weeks. He frequently had full gang meetings of these other regular contacts, and made sure that no quarrels were left to fester and destroy the overall cohesion. O'Hanlon was fully aware of how important it was to look after the men's welfare. One time he became ill and lost the power of his limbs for some weeks. In a similarly helpless situation, many lesser men might have lost control of the gang. This did not happen to O'Hanlon. He continued to issue instructions from his sick bed, and was looked after in a safe house by some of the local villagers.

As soon as he had regained his health, he took to the road again, but was captured one night while sleeping. Fortunately for him, his men attacked the military escort taking him to prison, and managed to release him. Following his escape, he returned to his old hide-out on Slieve Gullion where he continued to supervise his business of removing excess cash and valuables from all and sundry.

He was audacious to the point of recklessness.

He rode into Armagh one day dressed as an old country gentleman, and proceeded to transact some business. When he was ready to return home, he called at the local military barracks and asked for an escort to protect him from a possible attack by the outlaw O'Hanlon. He claimed that he was carrying a substantial amount of money and feared for his life. Following some negotiation about payment, his request was granted. The military commander had no reason to question the well-spoken gentleman with a very definite English accent. Some miles along the road, O'Hanlon even bought his escort some ale as an expression of his gratitude. When the soldiers had finished drinking, they could barely see each other, much less keep an eye out for rapparees.

It was the chance for which O'Hanlon had been waiting, and he whistled a signal to his men hiding near by. The gang had little trouble in overpowering the escort and taking their horses, weapons and any spare cash that they were carrying.

O'Hanlon took great pleasure in making the army look foolish, and he stole arms and supplies from them on several occasions. He even managed to sell them back their own stolen animals during a period of intense activity by the patrols. He swooped down on a temporary barracks near the

Monaghan border in south Armagh one night and over-powered the guards. His men proceeded to steal eighteen horses and made off with them. The alarm was raised and the army gave chase.

Knowing the country as well as he did, O'Hanlon pick-ed his spot carefully and allowed the pursuers to catch up with his men. The officer in charge of the army was delight-ed at what seemed to be the imminent capture of the out-laws. What he did not realise was that O'Hanlon had ar-ranged for other members of his gang to remain in hiding, and in fact had drawn the army into an ambush.

Realising that his entire company could be killed, the commander tried to negotiate, offering to call off hostilities if the horses were returned. O'Hanlon, being in a strong posi-tion, offered to return the horses at a price of one guinea each. At first the officer tried to bluff his way out of the situation by claiming that reinforcements were on their way and that he was really offering the outlaws a chance to save their lives. O'Hanlon increased his demands and directed that the troops surrender their weapons as well as pay the ransom for the horses. Eventually, the officer realised that he was not going to win, and agreed to the terms. The ransom was paid, and O'Hanlon and his men took the stolen horses and those belonging to the patrol, and left them about a mile away, where they were later collected by the soldiers.

Such actions did not enhance O'Hanlon's popularity with the army. The reward for his capture, dead or alive, was doubled. Military outposts were set up at several locations, and the hills thoroughly combed by the patrols. In a desperate attempt to buy information, a price was put on his head of £400, a fortune in those days.

O'Hanlon was still not betrayed.

Folklore and legend appear to agree on at least one fact. The authorities tried to lure O'Hanlon out of the hills by offering him a pardon. This was offered to him on condition that he agree to give evidence against Archbishop Plunkett in what became known as the Popish Plot. The outlaw refused to become involved in the scheme.

It is also claimed that the parish priest of Killevy spoke out against law-breakers and advised local people not to harbour outlaws like O'Hanlon. It was rash advice to give people who regarded the outlaw as a hero. The 'Captain' retaliated by warning everyone to stay away from Mass.

He stated that anyone who disobeyed him would lose one cow. A second visit to Mass would cost two cows, and a third visit would cost a life. One man who put the warning to the test was taken out of his house one night and murdered. No one else took his place at Mass. The priest later moved to another parish.

It was around this time that Cormacke Raver O'Murphy decided to challenge O'Hanlon for the leadership and was thrown out of the gang (see chapter four).

O'Murphy's short life was a grim indication that times were harsh and retribution swift. He had neither the skills nor the charm of O'Hanlon, for whom the people did seem to have a genuine regard. On the whole, he ensured that they were not robbed by rapparees, and there is no record of violence being used by him on those who paid the levy. It seems not unreasonable to assume that it was their regard that protected O'Hanlon from betrayal for all those years.

It has been claimed that O'Hanlon raised more money from his territory than that collected by the king's men for hearth money. Part of this income was paid out again in bribes to clerks and officials who in turn gave him vital information about movement of money, travellers and military actions. So well known was O'Hanlon by now that some reports of him had been circulating in French pamphlets where he became known as 'Count' O'Hanlon.

In September 1679 Mr Henry St John, owner of the castle and estate at Tandragee, went out riding with some friends. He was a wealthy man who had refused to pay protection money to O'Hanlon and had never paid for the return of any animals the outlaws had stolen. In fact, he was an enthusiastic tory hunter, and his son had died from pneumonia after a period of tory hunting. By a coincidence, Mr St John now owned a large portion of the old O'Hanlon territory.

On that particular September afternoon his ride was interrupted by a group of outlaws, who, acting under O'Hanlon's orders, attempted to kidnap Mr St John. Their victim, a man of some courage, refused to co-operate with his kidnappers. In the ensuing struggle, he was shot dead.

His murder galvanised the authorities into even more concentrated efforts to catch the outlaws. However, for the most part, the gang roamed almost at will, responding quickly and decisively to any attempt to capture them. One young man was so angry at his parents being robbed that he gave chase to the thieves as they left his home, and managed to recover some of the stolen property that the departing thieves had dropped. The outlaws returned during the early hours of the morning and burned down the house.

An informer told of a plot by O'Hanlon and his men to travel to Longford where he would meet up with sixteen other outlaws from Derry and Tyrone. It was, it seemed, their intention to rob a Widow Cope's house at Loughall. Because of poor planning by the army, the ambush was bungled and the outlaws escaped unscathed.

An interesting claim is made that O'Hanlon met another well known rapparee from Cork, called 'Captain' Power.

It seems that life was getting tough for 'Captain' Power and he decided to 'disappear' for a while. He had heard of O'Hanlon and decided to try and meet him. He crossed into Armagh and by chance the two men met. Their initial contact was not friendly and they fought a duel for half an hour with neither gaining the advantage. Unhurt, but tired and dusty, they agreed to rest, and discovered that they had more in common than a desire to rob or kill each other.

They became friends and Power rode with O'Hanlon for some months before heading home again. The decision almost cost him his life. He was captured and placed in Clonmel gaol. O'Hanlon heard about his capture and, ignoring advice from his men, immediately set out to help his friend. He arrived the day before Power was to be executed and managed to free him by getting the guards drunk and opening the cell doors while they slept. Alas, O'Hanlon could not persuade him to return to Ulster and relative safety. Power was not at home in the north and decided to remain where he felt he would be safer. He knew the terrain and was convinced that he had enough friends in the area to protect him.

Power managed to evade capture for some time, but he became careless. He was finally trapped and captured, and this time there was no escape from the gallows. O'Hanlon was not the type of man to leave any of his friends in danger and made another attempt to save Power, but the news of his friend's capture was late in reaching him, and he arrived too late to change the course of history.

Back in Ulster again, he continued to pile success upon success, and the authorities became desperate in their attempts to trap him. Tory hunting was a profitable business for many people. These early day 'bounty hunters' were not always very careful when it came to distinguishing between a tory and a perfectly innocent man. A number of lonely travellers were stopped and beheaded, not by outlaws, but by over-enthusiastic tory hunters, who proceeded to present the heads to the authorities, claiming them to belong to some minor tories, and pocket the head money.

Along with all the fame and glory, came greater difficulty in avoiding escape. O'Hanlon's pursuers were now more numerous than ever, and he was getting tired. At forty years of age, he was old for an outlaw, and the responsibility of leadership was a heavy burden. Thoughts of retirement or even a pardon must have entered his head when fatigue was too much for him. He was not without friends in high places who could have used their influence on his behalf.

On 6 October 1680 the Bishop of Clogher in a letter to Primate Boyle, arguing for a pardon for O'Hanlon and his brother, wrote, '... as for the matter of murthers, I doubt they would be found guilty of several, but I never heard they killed but in their own defence ... and murthers have been pardoned. If anything can be done for them, I beg your Grace to signify it'.

Deborah Annesley, daughter of the Bishop of Meath, presented her father with a petition on O'Hanlon's behalf and asked him to place it before the Privy Council. It received little sympathy. The bishop's reply was:

> ... my orders are to assure him of a pardon on ye terms formerly proposed – his declaring himself, and assuring the government of his reality in first bringing in or cutting off some of ye heads of ye principal Toreys, such as are proclaimed or known to be such. After which, the pardon shall be for him and his friends, they undertaking to free the country of Toreys....

Mrs Annesley wrote to O'Hanlon informing him that because he would not betray his friends, there would be no
pardon, and that the Privy Council had increased the reward
money on him and his brother. However, the bishop then
sent a message through his daughter to O'Hanlon, suggesting that it would be worth the outlaw's while if he 'came
over to me'. He promised O'Hanlon a pardon if he would
turn king's evidence against Archbishop Plunkett. The bishop believed that the outlaw knew all about the planned invasion, and he secretly hoped to persuade O'Hanlon to travel to London as a witness. The outlaw may well have been
aware that the bishop was anxious to prove Archbishop
Oliver Plunkett's complicity in a French invasion, and he refused to have any part in such treachery. He continued to
live in the Slieve Gullion, Forkhill district where he trusted
the people not to betray him.

More soldiers were now employed in searching for
O'Hanlon in Co. Armagh than in searching for all of the
other outlaws put together.

Travelling was almost as hazardous for the outlaws as it
was for the unsuspecting traveller. O'Hanlon's men continued to operate effectively and loyally. They were still collecting the annual levy from the farmers, but they were now
also finding it more difficult to extract the money. Whether
through fear of retaliation by the military, or a hardening of
attitude against the outlaws, people were beginning to refuse to give over the money. This resistance, together with
the ever-increasing success of military patrols, began to de-
plete seriously the number of men at O'Hanlon's disposal.
Several of his most trusted followers had been shot. The
people who had happily taken bribes in return for information, were now also finding it difficult to operate. They were

not always able to make contact with him in time to prevent a clash with army patrols.

This breakdown in communication led to many close shaves for the gang. O'Hanlon rode with a group of his men into an area where the military was patrolling and made his getaway only after a lengthy gun battle. On another occasion he was resting in what he regarded as a safe house when the military arrived to search it. He tried to get away without leaving the tenants in any danger, but was spotted as he reached the cover of nearby trees. A cordon was placed around the place where he had been seen, and an immediate search was implemented. For the next two days the troops searched the area but they failed to find him, and in the end they were withdrawn and he made his escape.

An arranged meeting with an informer almost resulted in disaster for the outlaw when the military came upon him waiting in the woods. It was only his ability to speak French which helped him to convince the soldiers that he was an innocent Frenchman, allowing him to make a getaway.

Slowly and inexorably the authorities were closing in on him. In all probability, men of O'Hanlon's calibre fully realised how little chance they had of remaining free. It was always on the cards that the end of a rope on some gallows would be their ultimate destiny. They accepted that end as part and parcel of everyday life.

Some, like O'Hanlon, were never pardoned, and survived relatively long because of their ability to plan their operations, and remain one step ahead of the military. The life of a highwayman was far from glamorous. During the summer the outlaws were at least able to keep themselves warm, and food was easier to obtain. During the winter, wet and cold, the men must have wished to be anywhere but hiding out in some cave on a windswept mountain.

For over twenty years O'Hanlon had lived outside the law, answerable only to himself. For most of that time fifty men had followed his orders and risked their lives carrying out his orders. He still felt responsible for them. Yet he was tired of being on the run.

The irony of the situation, and O'Hanlon must have been aware of it, was that realistically there was no future for any of them. Even retirement was full of the danger of being recognised and reported. There was no escape, no pardon, no peace. He was known in tale and song far beyond the shores of Ulster, and hundreds of soldiers were every day combing the hills for him. His petition for a pardon had been refused and the authorities were unlikely to reverse their decision. His very success had made it impossible to give up his profession. As a highwayman he lived – and a highwayman he would die.

The raids continued.

O'Hanlon had outwitted the military for so long that he might well have been happy to know that he would cheat the gallows. The events that finally led to his death are not entirely clear. What is certain, however, is that credit for the plan which led to his demise is claimed by two parties.

For some time, it had been the Duke of Ormonde's ambition to end the career of the tory. He was convinced that the usual methods of military procedures and patrols were too cumbersome ever to bring the outlaw to justice. He also knew that O'Hanlon had so many friends and spies throughout the county, that only a trusted friend and colleague would ever get close enough to take his head. It had come to the duke's attention that a man called Art O'Hanlon, a foster brother of the outlaw, worked for a Mr William

Lucas of Drumintyne. Sources close to the duke had also stated that Art had been known to ride with the outlaws.

Thus, the duke, with the aid of Mr Lucas, persuaded Art to betray his foster brother, or himself face proclamation and death as a tory. No doubt Art had little difficulty in accepting the commission when he was guaranteed his life, a pardon and a reward if he co-operated with the authorities.

Sir Toby Poyntz has also claimed the credit for the plan which led to the end of O'Hanlon. It seems that Art O'Hanlon had been employed by Sir Charles Poyntz, a relative of Sir Toby, and in a letter Sir Toby claims that he persuaded Art to kill Redmond and his brother, Loughlin.

Whoever worked out the details of the plan is of little importance after three hundred years. Art O'Hanlon turned out to be the villain – that much is certain.

Following the instructions of his paymaster, Art joined O'Hanlon's gang on a full-time basis and was soon, probably because of his relationship to the 'Captain', one of his bodyguard when he was away from the main body of the gang, on a scouting mission, or meeting informants.

On Monday, 25 April 1681, O'Hanlon and two men occupied an empty cabin while they waited for Loughlin and the rest of the gang to join them. The 'Captain' had been awake most of the previous night making plans for another raid and decided to take the chance of some sleep. One of his bodyguards, William O'Sheil, kept watch outside the cabin some distance along the road, while his colleague, Art O'Hanlon, remained with their sleeping leader.

It was the chance for which Art had been waiting. He fired the contents of a loaded blunderbuss into Redmond's chest, and left immediately to find the soldiers who had been directed into the area. He was aware that any of the

gang would cut his throat if they got to him before he reached the protection of the military.

O'Sheil, on hearing the noise, reached the cabin to find
the dying figure of O'Hanlon who ordered him to behead
him when he had died to prevent his head from falling into
the hands of the enemy. This O'Sheil did and concealed the
head in an old unused well. He then alerted Loughlin and
the others to avoid the area. When the military arrived they
took O'Hanlon's body into Newry, and men were sent out to
search for the head. Some days later it was found and duly
spiked outside Downpatrick gaol.

His remains were later given to his family and he was
buried in the graveyard of Ballynabeck, close to the road
from Tandragee to Scarva. Art O'Hanlon received £100.

Loughlin, having escaped capture, continued to lead the
gang, with the help of another brother, Edmund. Neither of
them had the qualities of Redmond, and this seemed to be
recognised by their grandparents who asked that they be
pardoned. While this was being considered, Loughlin was
killed by Mr John Mullin, who received £50 as a reward.

The gang of Redmond O'Hanlon was lost without him.
Soon the head of Shane Hagan was placed before the military. Then Lieutenant Lucas wrote to Sir Francis Brewster on
20 May 1681 that, '... last night I brought in the head of Cor-
mick McCarren, who I shot myself. He has been a thief ever
since he was able to crawl and has robbed this two years
past, and I do assure you, he was one that pestered this
county mightily....'

Within a few weeks, six outlaws from the old gang had
been taken, and when Edmund finally received his pardon,
the remainder of the gang decided to move into Co. Tyrone.

Unfortunately for them, the people of Tyrone seemed

much less friendly than those of Armagh, and gradually the gang split up as members went their own way or were caught by tory hunters or the army.

'Count' Redmond O'Hanlon strode into the annals of folklore and myth, and time has been kind to him. Historians have disagreed about his actual burial place, and suggestions were put forward that he was laid to rest in Donegal and not Armagh. Then, one day in August 1937, five men unearthed a slab in the graveyard of the old Church of Ireland in Church Street, Letterkenny. For the previous two weeks the men had been engaged in excavation work in the graveyard, and when the great slab had been washed clean, the inscription could be read fairly easily. It read:

> Here lieth the bodeys of the five sons of
> Redmond Hanlon 'March' in Letterkenny;
> John, the first-born; Alexander, Frances,
> John and Redmond.
> Also here lieth the body of William
> Hanlon, son of the aforesaid Redmond
> Hanlon, who departed this life on the
> 27th day of May ano 1708, aged 13 years
> 10 months and 11 days.

Those who made the discovery were George Cannen, Town Clerk; E.C.H. Knox, Collector of Taxes; James Kelly, UDC; Patrick Goban, Town Clerk; and a local journalist.

The 'William Hanlon' is thought to be a grandson of the 'Count'. While it is curious that no mention is made of Redmond himself, tradition has always maintained that he shared a grave with his five sons. Perhaps it was decided not to have his name on the stone because of his occupation. No one will ever know. Few could compare with him as a highwayman. It is perhaps fitting that he has left us with a question which, so far, remains unanswered.